SCOTLAND TRAVEL GUIDE ATLAS ROAD MAP 2024/2025

Exploring The Beauty Of Edinburgh, Glasgow, Highlands, And Isle Of Skye And Discover Hidden Places With Travel Practical Tips

STEVES GUIDE

Contents

INTRODUCTION

Scotland is where ancient history, vibrant culture, and breathtaking landscapes converge to create an unforgettable travel experience. From its misty highlands and rugged coastlines to its bustling cities and serene lochs, Scotland offers a diverse array of sights, sounds, and experiences that captivate the hearts of travellers worldwide.

One of the first things you'll notice about Scotland is its deep-rooted sense of history. Every corner of this country tells a story. Whether it's the haunting echoes of battles fought long ago, the majestic castles that have stood the test of time, or the timeless traditions that continue to thrive in modern Scottish life. Scotland's history is woven into the fabric of its culture, influencing everything from its music and dance to its language and cuisine.

Speaking of culture, Scotland is a vibrant tapestry of traditions and modernity. The country's cultural heritage is rich and diverse, with influences from Celtic, Norse, and even Roman civilizations. This blend of influences has given rise to a unique cultural identity, one that is proudly celebrated through festivals, music, and the arts. The annual Edinburgh Festival Fringe, the world's largest arts festival, is just one example of how Scotland continues to be a global hub for creativity and innovation.

But it's not just history and culture that make Scotland special—it's the landscapes. Scotland's natural beauty is legendary, with dramatic mountains, tranquil lochs, and wild coastlines that offer some of the most spectacular scenery in the world. The Highlands, with their rugged peaks and deep glens, are a hiker's paradise, while the islands of the Hebrides and Orkney offer remote and unspoiled beauty that feels like a step back in time. Whether you're exploring the rolling hills of the Borders, the lush forests of Perthshire, or the windswept beaches of the Outer Hebrides, you'll find that Scotland's landscapes are as varied as they are stunning.

And then there's the people. The Scots are known for their warmth, hospitality, and fierce pride in their heritage. Whether you're sharing a dram of whisky in a cosy pub, learning about local history from a passionate guide, or simply enjoying the friendly banter with locals, you'll find that the people of Scotland are what truly make this country feel like home.

In Scotland, you'll find a destination that is not only steeped in tradition but also constantly evolving. It's a place where ancient landscapes meet modern cities, where the past is always present but never overpowering, and where every traveller can find something that speaks to their soul. Whether you're here to trace your ancestry, explore the great outdoors, or immerse yourself in the vibrant culture, Scotland is a place that will leave a lasting impression on you.

What's New in 2024

As Scotland continues to embrace its rich history while evolving with the times, 2024 brings exciting new attractions, events, and changes to its tourism landscape. Whether you're a returning visitor eager to discover what's new or a first-timer looking to experience the latest offerings, this section will guide you through the highlights that make Scotland in 2024 an even more captivating destination.

1. New Attractions and Experiences

a. The Edinburgh Castle Virtual Reality Experience

In 2024, Edinburgh Castle, one of Scotland's most iconic landmarks, is introducing a state-of-the-art Virtual Reality (VR) experience. This immersive attraction allows visitors to step back in time and witness historical events as they unfold within the castle walls. From medieval battles to royal ceremonies, the VR experience offers a dynamic and educational way to explore Scotland's history like never before. Whether you're a history buff or just curious about the past, this new addition to Edinburgh Castle is a must-see.

b. The Stirling Castle Renaissance Garden

Stirling Castle has unveiled its Renaissance Garden, meticulously restored to reflect its appearance in the 16th century. This garden is not only a beautiful place to explore but also offers insight into the horticultural practices and aesthetic sensibilities of Scotland's Renaissance period. The garden features historically accurate plant species, ornamental designs, and even a recreated fountain that was once the pride of the castle grounds. Guided tours and interactive displays provide a deeper understanding of the role gardens played in royal life during the Renaissance.

c. The Outer Hebrides Coastal Path

Scotland's renowned natural beauty is on full display with the opening of the Outer Hebrides Coastal Path. This new long-distance trail stretches over 200 miles, linking the islands from Barra to Lewis. It offers hikers a unique opportunity to explore some of Scotland's most remote and untouched landscapes, with stunning coastal views, pristine beaches, and a chance to observe the rich wildlife that inhabits these islands. Whether you're an avid hiker or prefer shorter walks, the Outer Hebrides Coastal Path is set to become a highlight for nature lovers visiting Scotland.

d. The Glasgow Art District

Glasgow, already known for its vibrant arts scene, has launched its new Art District in 2024. This dedicated area in the heart of the city showcases contemporary art galleries, open studios, and public art installations, celebrating the creativity and innovation of local and international artists. The district also hosts regular events, workshops, and exhibitions, making it a dynamic space for both art enthusiasts and casual visitors to immerse themselves in Scotland's contemporary culture.

2. Major Events and Festivals

a. The Edinburgh International Festival 2024

The Edinburgh International Festival, already one of the world's most prestigious arts events, promises an even more spectacular lineup in 2024. This year's festival will focus on celebrating Scotland's connections with the global arts community, featuring collaborations with artists from around the world. Expect cutting-edge performances in theatre, music, dance, and visual arts, along with special events that explore themes of cultural exchange and innovation. The festival is also expanding its reach with outdoor performances and interactive installations throughout the city, making it more accessible and inclusive than ever before.

b. The Highland Games 2024

The Highland Games, a cherished Scottish tradition, are getting a fresh twist in 2024. New events have been introduced that blend traditional athletic contests with modern sports, offering something for everyone. In addition to the classic caber toss and tug-of-war, visitors can now participate in or watch events like trail running, mountain biking, and even drone racing, all set against the stunning backdrop of the Scottish

Highlands. The games are also embracing technology with enhanced live-streaming options, allowing fans worldwide to join in the excitement.

c. The Orkney Viking Festival

2024 sees the inaugural Orkney Viking Festival, a celebration of Orkney's Norse heritage. This new festival promises to be a highlight of the Scottish events calendar, with a week of activities that include Viking reenactments, boat races, traditional crafts, and storytelling. The festival will also feature educational workshops that delve into the history of the Viking presence in Orkney, making it both a fun and informative experience for all ages. The Orkney Viking Festival is sure to become a beloved annual tradition, attracting history enthusiasts and families alike.

3. Changes in Scotland's Tourism Landscape

a. Sustainable Tourism Initiatives

In 2024, Scotland continues its commitment to sustainable tourism, with several new initiatives aimed at preserving the country's natural beauty while enhancing the visitor experience. The Scottish government has introduced the "Leave No Trace" campaign, which encourages responsible travel practices, such as minimizing waste, respecting wildlife, and supporting local communities. Many tourist sites have also adopted eco-friendly measures, including reduced plastic use, renewable energy sources, and programs that support biodiversity conservation. Travellers can now participate in volunteer opportunities focused on environmental conservation, offering a hands-on way to give back while enjoying Scotland's natural wonders.

b. Enhanced Transportation Options

Getting around Scotland is easier than ever in 2024, thanks to improvements in public transportation and new travel options designed to make exploring the country more convenient. The launch of Scotland's new high-speed rail line between Edinburgh and Inverness significantly reduces travel time, making it easier to visit multiple destinations in a single trip. Additionally, a new fleet of electric buses has been introduced in major cities, providing a more sustainable way to explore urban areas. For those looking to venture off the beaten path, car rental companies are offering more eco-friendly vehicles, including hybrids and electric cars, helping travellers reduce their carbon footprint.

c. The Rise of Agritourism

Agritourism is becoming increasingly popular in Scotland, with 2024 seeing a significant rise in farm stays, farm-to-table dining experiences, and agricultural tours. Visitors can now immerse themselves in rural Scottish life by staying on working farms, participating in activities like sheep shearing, cheese making, and foraging, and enjoying meals made from the freshest local ingredients. This trend not only offers a unique travel experience but also supports Scotland's agricultural communities and promotes sustainable food practices. Whether you're a foodie, a nature lover, or simply looking for a tranquil retreat, Scotland's agritourism scene is worth exploring.

d. New Accommodation Options

Scotland's accommodation scene is evolving to meet the needs of today's travellers, with new options ranging from luxury eco-lodges to unique glamping experiences. In 2024, several new boutique hotels have opened in Edinburgh, Glasgow, and the Highlands, offering a blend of modern amenities and traditional Scottish charm. For those seeking something different, new glamping sites have popped up in picturesque locations, providing a more immersive experience in nature without sacrificing comfort. Whether you're looking for a five-star hotel in the city or a cosy cabin in the wilderness, Scotland's accommodation options in 2024 cater to every taste and budget.

CHAPTER 1

SCOTLAND AT A GLANCE

Geography and Regions

Scotland, a country renowned for its breathtaking landscapes, rich history, and vibrant culture, offers an extraordinary range of geographical diversity that captivates visitors from all over the world. From the rugged, mountainous Highlands to the rolling hills of the Lowlands, each region of Scotland has its unique character and charm. In this chapter, we'll explore the key geographical features and regions that make Scotland such a fascinating destination.

1. The Highlands

The Highlands of Scotland are perhaps the most iconic and recognizable part of the country. Known for their dramatic landscapes, the Highlands are characterized by towering mountains, deep glens, and expansive lochs. This region is sparsely populated, with small villages and towns scattered across the rugged terrain. The Highlands are also home to Ben Nevis, the highest peak in the British Isles, standing at 4,413 feet.

The Highlands offer a sense of wild beauty and untamed nature that is hard to find elsewhere. This region is a paradise for outdoor enthusiasts, with countless opportunities for hiking, climbing, and exploring. The North Coast 500, often referred to as Scotland's answer to Route 66, is a popular driving route that takes travellers on a stunning journey around the northernmost part of the Highlands, showcasing some of the most breathtaking scenery in the country.

The Highlands are also steeped in history and legend, with many ancient castles, battlefields, and monuments dotting the landscape. The area is closely associated with the clans of Scotland, and visitors can learn about the clan system and the region's turbulent history at various heritage sites.

2. The Lowlands

In contrast to the Highlands, the Lowlands of Scotland are characterized by gentler, rolling hills, fertile plains, and a more temperate climate. The Lowlands are the most populous region of Scotland, encompassing major cities such as Edinburgh, Glasgow, and Stirling. Despite the region's name, the Lowlands are not entirely flat; they include some notable hills and ranges, such as the Pentland Hills near Edinburgh.

The Lowlands are often seen as the cultural and economic heart of Scotland. Edinburgh, the capital city, is known for its stunning architecture, historic landmarks, and vibrant arts scene. The city's medieval Old Town and Georgian New Town are UNESCO World Heritage Sites, offering a glimpse into Scotland's rich history and architectural heritage. Edinburgh is also famous for hosting the world's largest arts festival, the Edinburgh Festival Fringe, which attracts performers and audiences from around the globe each summer.

Glasgow, Scotland's largest city, is another major cultural hub. Known for its Victorian and art nouveau architecture, Glasgow boasts a lively music scene, world-class museums, and a strong sense of local identity. The city's history as an industrial powerhouse has given way to a modern, cosmopolitan atmosphere, making it a must-visit destination for those interested in contemporary Scottish culture.

Stirling, often referred to as the "Gateway to the Highlands," is a city rich in history. Its most famous landmark, Stirling Castle, played a pivotal role in Scotland's history, particularly during the Wars of Scottish Independence. The nearby Bannockburn battlefield, where Robert the Bruce defeated the English army in 1314, is another significant historical site.

3. The Isle of Skye

The Isle of Skye, located off the west coast of Scotland, is one of the most popular destinations for visitors to the country. Known for its rugged landscapes, dramatic coastlines, and rich history, Skye offers a truly unique experience. The island is part of the Inner Hebrides and is connected to the mainland by the Skye Bridge.

Skye is famous for its natural beauty, with highlights including the Cuillin mountain range, the Quiraing landslip, and the Old Man of Storr. These geological formations create some of the most photographed landscapes in Scotland. The island is also home to several picturesque villages, such as Portree, the island's main town, which is known for its colourful harbour and traditional charm.

Skye's history is as compelling as its scenery. The island has been inhabited since prehistoric times, and it has a rich Gaelic heritage that is still evident today. Visitors can explore ancient ruins, castles, and standing stones that tell the story of Skye's past. The island's history is also marked by the Jacobite uprisings, with sites such as the Armadale Castle and Museum of the Isles offering insights into this turbulent period.

Skye is also a haven for wildlife, with opportunities to see otters, seals, eagles, and even whales along the coast. The island's diverse ecosystems make it a great destination for nature lovers and those interested in Scotland's natural heritage.

4. The Scottish Borders

The Scottish Borders, located in the southeastern part of Scotland, is a region known for its rolling hills, lush countryside, and rich history. This area is often overlooked by tourists, but it offers a wealth of attractions and a more tranquil experience compared to the busier regions of Scotland.

The Borders have a long history of conflict, particularly during the medieval period when the region was frequently caught in the crossfire between Scotland and England. The remnants of this turbulent history can be seen in the many castles, abbeys, and fortified houses that dot the landscape. Remarkable sites include Melrose Abbey, Jedburgh Abbey, and the impressive Floors Castle.

The region is also known for its textiles, particularly its production of high-quality tweed. The town of Hawick, often referred to as the home of tweed, has a rich history in the textile industry, and visitors can learn about this at the local museums and mills.

The Scottish Borders are ideal for those who enjoy outdoor activities. The region offers excellent opportunities for walking, cycling, and fishing, with scenic routes such as the Southern Upland Way and the Borders Abbeys Way providing a chance to explore the countryside at a leisurely pace.

5. The Orkney and Shetland Islands

Located off the northern coast of mainland Scotland, the Orkney and Shetland Islands offer a stark contrast to the rest of the country. These remote archipelagos are known for their dramatic coastal landscapes, unique wildlife, and rich archaeological sites.

Orkney is particularly famous for its Neolithic sites, which are among the best-preserved in Europe. The UNESCO World Heritage Site known as the Heart of Neolithic Orkney includes the ancient village of Skara Brae, the Ring of Brodgar stone circle, and the Maeshowe chambered cairn. These sites provide a fascinating glimpse into the lives of Scotland's earliest inhabitants.

Shetland, further to the north, is known for its rugged beauty and strong Norse heritage. The islands were once part of the Viking world, and this influence is still evident in the local culture, place names, and archaeological sites. Shetland is also home to some of the best wildlife-watching opportunities in Scotland, with seabird colonies, seals, and orcas frequently spotted along the coast.

Both Orkney and Shetland offer a more isolated and peaceful experience, making them ideal destinations for those looking to escape the hustle and bustle of mainland Scotland.

Climate and Best Times to Visit

Scotland's weather is famously unpredictable, but understanding the country's climate patterns can significantly enhance your travel experience. In this section, we'll delve into Scotland's weather throughout the year, providing insights into what you can expect in each season and offering recommendations on the best times to visit based on your interests and activities.

1. Overview of Scotland's Climate

Scotland's climate is classified as temperate maritime, influenced by the Atlantic Ocean and the Gulf Stream. This means the country experiences relatively mild temperatures year-round, with no extreme heat in summer or intense cold in winter. However, the weather can change rapidly, often featuring four seasons in a single day.

The western regions, particularly the Highlands and islands, are generally wetter and milder due to their proximity to the Atlantic. The eastern regions, such as Aberdeenshire and the Borders, tend to be drier and cooler. Coastal areas are generally windier, while the inland regions, especially the Highlands, can experience more significant temperature variations.

2. Seasons in Scotland

Spring (March to May):

Spring in Scotland is a time of renewal, with the landscape coming to life after the long winter. Temperatures during this season range from 6°C to 15°C (43°F to 59°F), with gradually lengthening days and blooming flowers adding vibrant colours to the scenery. Spring is an excellent time to visit if you enjoy walking or hiking, as the weather is usually mild, and the countryside is lush and green. However, rain showers are still common, so be prepared for wet weather.

Spring is also a time of festivals and events, such as the Edinburgh International Science Festival and the Spirit of Speyside Whisky Festival. These events offer unique opportunities to experience Scotland's culture and traditions.

Summer (June to August):

Summer is the most popular time to visit Scotland, as the weather is generally the warmest and driest of the year. Temperatures typically range from 10°C to 19°C (50°F to 66°F), with occasional heatwaves pushing temperatures into the mid-20s Celsius (70s Fahrenheit). The long daylight hours, known as the "White Nights" in the north, allow for extended exploration, with the sun setting as late as 11 pm in some areas.

Summer is the ideal time for outdoor activities, such as hiking, cycling, and exploring Scotland's many castles and historic sites. The festivals in Edinburgh, including the Edinburgh International Festival and the Fringe, draw huge crowds and offer a cultural feast. However, summer is also the peak tourist season, so popular destinations can be crowded, and accommodation prices may be higher.

One downside of summer in Scotland is the presence of midges, tiny biting insects that are particularly troublesome in the Highlands and around lochs. While they are more of an annoyance than a serious threat, it's worth bringing insect repellent if you plan to spend time outdoors in these areas.

Autumn (September to November):

Autumn in Scotland is a season of stunning natural beauty, with the countryside transforming into a tapestry of reds, oranges, and yellows. Temperatures during autumn are cooler, ranging from 5°C to 14°C (41°F to 57°F), and the weather can be quite variable, with a mix of sunny days and rain showers.

This season is perfect for those who prefer a quieter, more peaceful experience, as the summer crowds have dispersed, and many popular tourist spots are less busy. Autumn is also the time of the deer rutting season in the Highlands, which is a spectacular sight for wildlife enthusiasts.

Cultural events, such as the Royal National Mod, Scotland's premier Gaelic cultural festival, take place in autumn, offering visitors a chance to immerse themselves in Scotland's linguistic and musical heritage.

Winter (December to February):

Winter in Scotland is characterized by short days, long nights, and cold temperatures, ranging from 0°C to 7°C (32°F to 45°F). Snow is common in the Highlands and other elevated areas, making this season ideal for winter sports enthusiasts. Skiing and snowboarding are popular activities in Scotland's ski resorts, such as Glenshee, Cairngorm Mountain, and Nevis Range.

While the weather can be harsh, winter also has its charms. The cities, particularly Edinburgh and Glasgow, are beautifully illuminated with festive lights during the holiday season, and events like Hogmanay (New Year's Eve) are celebrated with great enthusiasm. Visiting Scotland in winter offers a chance to experience the country's landscapes in a different light, with frost-covered hills and snow-dusted castles creating a magical atmosphere.

However, winter travel in Scotland requires careful planning, as some remote areas may be inaccessible due to snow, and daylight hours are limited. It's advisable to have a flexible itinerary and be prepared for potential weather-related disruptions.

3. Best Times to Visit Based on Activities

For Outdoor Adventures:

If your primary goal is to explore Scotland's natural landscapes through hiking, cycling, or wildlife watching, the best times to visit are late spring (May to June) and early autumn (September to October). During these months, the weather is generally mild, the landscapes are vibrant, and the midges are less of a problem than in peak summer.

For Festivals and Cultural Events:

Scotland is known for its vibrant cultural scene, with numerous festivals and events taking place throughout the year. The summer months, particularly August, are ideal for experiencing Scotland's festivals, including the Edinburgh International Festival, the Fringe, and the Royal Edinburgh Military Tattoo. However, if you prefer a quieter cultural experience, visiting during the shoulder seasons of spring and autumn can also be rewarding, with events such as the Beltane Fire Festival in April and the Scottish International Storytelling Festival in October.

For Winter Sports:

Winter sports enthusiasts should plan their visit between December and February when Scotland's ski resorts are in full swing. The Cairngorms and the Highlands offer some of the best skiing and snowboarding opportunities in the UK, with a range of slopes suitable for all skill levels.

For Photography and Scenic Drives:

Scotland's dramatic landscapes are a photographer's dream, and the best times for capturing the country's natural beauty are during the golden hours of early morning and late afternoon in the autumn. The autumnal colours, combined with the soft light of the season, create stunning photo opportunities. Scenic drives, such as the North Coast 500 and the A82 through Glencoe, are particularly picturesque in autumn, with the changing leaves adding to the visual appeal.

4. Final Tips for Visiting Scotland

No matter when you choose to visit Scotland, it's essential to be prepared for the possibility of unpredictable weather. Packing layers, waterproof clothing, and sturdy footwear is always a good idea, as you may encounter rain, wind, and chilly temperatures at any time of year. Additionally, Scotland's weather can vary significantly from one region to another, so it's wise to check the forecast for your specific destination before heading out.

Cultural Highlights:

Scotland's cultural heritage is as rich and varied as its landscapes, reflecting centuries of history, a vibrant mix of traditions, and a deep connection to its past. From the ancient Gaelic language to the famous Highland games, Scotland's culture offers visitors a unique and immersive experience. In this section, we'll explore the key elements that define Scotland's cultural identity, including its language, traditions, festivals, and cuisine.

1. Language

Scotland is a multilingual country, with three official languages: English, Scots, and Gaelic. While English is the dominant language spoken throughout the country, Scots and Gaelic hold significant cultural importance.

English:

The version of English spoken in Scotland, often referred to as Scottish English, includes distinct vocabulary and pronunciation influenced by Scots. You'll notice words like "wee" (small), "bairn" (child), and "loch" (lake) in everyday conversations, reflecting the unique linguistic flavour of Scotland.

Scots:

Scots is a Germanic language closely related to English and is spoken by a significant portion of the population, particularly in the Lowlands. Scots have a rich literary tradition, with writers like Robert Burns and Sir Walter Scott contributing to its prominence. While not as widely spoken today, efforts to preserve and promote Scots continue through literature, music, and education.

Gaelic:

Scottish Gaelic, a Celtic language, has been spoken in Scotland for over 1,500 years and is still used, primarily in the Highlands and the Western Isles. Although the number of Gaelic speakers has declined, the language remains an integral part of Scottish identity. Gaelic is taught in schools, broadcast on television and radio, and celebrated through cultural events such as the Royal National Mod, a festival of Gaelic music, arts, and culture.

2. Traditions

Scotland's traditions are deeply rooted in its history and often revolve around community, music, and the land. These customs offer a window into the Scottish way of life, providing visitors with an authentic cultural experience.

Highland Games:

The Highland Games are one of Scotland's most famous traditions, dating back to the 11th century. These events, held across the country during the summer months, are a celebration of Scottish culture, featuring athletic competitions such as caber tossing, tug-of-war, and hammer throwing. The games also showcase traditional music, dance, and Highland dress, including the iconic kilt.

Ceilidh:

A ceilidh (pronounced "kay-lee") is a traditional Scottish social gathering featuring folk music, dancing, and storytelling. Ceilidhs are a lively and inclusive part of Scottish culture, often held to celebrate weddings, festivals, and other community events. The dances are usually simple and easy to learn, making them a fun way for visitors to engage with local culture.

Tartan and Kilts:

Tartan, a patterned cloth associated with Scottish clans, is a symbol of Scotland's heritage. Each clan has its distinctive tartan pattern, which is used to make kilts, sashes, and other garments. The kilt, traditionally worn by men, is a national symbol of pride and is often seen at formal events, Highland Games, and celebrations such as weddings.

Bagpipes:

The bagpipes are perhaps the most recognizable symbol of Scottish music. This ancient instrument, with its distinctive sound, has been a part of Scottish culture for centuries. Bagpipes are played at a wide range of events, from military ceremonies to weddings, and are a key feature of the Highland Games.

3. Festivals

Scotland is home to a rich calendar of festivals that celebrate everything from the arts and music to food and historical events. These festivals provide a vibrant showcase of Scottish culture and attract visitors from around the world.

Edinburgh Festivals:

Edinburgh, Scotland's capital, is renowned for its festivals, particularly in August when the city hosts the Edinburgh International Festival and the Edinburgh Festival Fringe. The International Festival features world-class performances in music, theatre, and dance, while the Fringe is the world's largest arts festival, offering a diverse range of shows, from comedy to experimental theatre.

Hogmanay:

Hogmanay, Scotland's New Year celebration, is legendary for its scale and enthusiasm. The festivities typically last for several days, with street parties, torchlight processions, and fireworks lighting up the night. Edinburgh's Hogmanay is one of the most famous, attracting thousands of visitors each year, but celebrations take place across the country, each with its local flavour.

Burns Night:

Burns Night, celebrated on January 25th, honours Scotland's national poet, Robert Burns. The evening typically involves a traditional Burns Supper, where guests enjoy haggis, recite Burns' poetry, and toast with whisky. Burns Night is a cherished event in Scotland, reflecting the enduring influence of the poet's work on Scottish culture.

Beltane Fire Festival:

Held on April 30th in Edinburgh, the Beltane Fire Festival is a modern interpretation of the ancient Celtic festival of Beltane. The event marks the beginning of summer with a vibrant display of fire, music, and performance, celebrating the themes of life, death, and rebirth. The festival offers a unique insight into Scotland's pagan heritage and is a must-see for those interested in alternative cultural experiences.

St. Andrew's Day:

St. Andrew's Day, celebrated on November 30th, is Scotland's national day, honouring its patron saint. The day is marked by various events, including traditional music, dancing, and food. In some areas, St. Andrew's Day is also seen as the start of the winter festival season, leading up to Christmas and Hogmanay.

4. Cuisine

Scottish cuisine is a reflection of the country's history, geography, and cultural influences. From hearty traditional dishes to innovative modern cuisine, Scotland offers a diverse culinary experience.

Haggis:

Haggis is Scotland's national dish, made from sheep's offal mixed with oatmeal, suet, and spices, traditionally encased in a sheep's stomach. It's often served with "neeps and tatties" (turnips and potatoes) and is a staple at Burns Suppers. While haggis may sound unusual to some, it's a flavourful and comforting dish that embodies Scotland's rustic culinary traditions.

Scottish Breakfast:

A traditional Scottish breakfast is a hearty affair, typically including items such as black pudding, Lorne sausage, tattie scones, eggs, bacon, and baked beans. It's the perfect way to start a day of exploring, providing plenty of energy for Scotland's rugged landscapes.

Seafood:

Scotland is renowned for its high-quality seafood, with salmon, haddock, and shellfish being particularly prized. Scottish salmon is internationally renowned, often enjoyed smoked or poached. Coastal towns and cities, such as Aberdeen and Oban, offer some of the freshest seafood, served in a variety of traditional and modern dishes.

Whisky:

Scotland's whisky, or "Scotch," is world-famous, with a history dating back over 500 years. There are five distinct whisky regions in Scotland: Highlands, Lowlands, Islay, Speyside, and Campbeltown, each producing whiskies with unique characteristics. Whisky distillery tours are a popular activity for visitors, offering a chance to learn about the distilling process and sample different varieties.

Cullen Skink:

Cullen skink is a traditional Scottish soup made from smoked haddock, potatoes, and onions. It's a rich, creamy dish that's particularly popular in the northeast of Scotland. Often served as a starter, it's a warming and satisfying meal, especially on a cold day.

Shortbread:

Shortbread is a classic Scottish biscuit made from butter, sugar, and flour. It's a simple yet delicious treat, often enjoyed with a cup of tea or given as a gift. The town of Edinburgh is particularly known for its high-quality shortbread, and you'll find it in many variations across the country.

Cranachan:

Cranachan is a traditional Scottish dessert made with whipped cream, honey, raspberries, toasted oats, and a splash of whisky. It's a light, fruity dessert that's perfect for finishing off a meal, particularly in the summer when raspberries are in season.

CHAPTER 2

PLANNING YOUR TRIP

When planning your journey to Scotland, there are several key travel essentials you'll want to get sorted ahead of time. This chapter will walk you through everything you need to know about visas, currency, language, health and safety tips, and travel insurance, ensuring that you're fully prepared for your Scottish adventure.

Visas and Entry Requirements

Scotland, as part of the United Kingdom, follows the UK's visa policies. For travellers from many countries, including the United States, Canada, Australia, and much of Europe, a visa isn't required for short stays of up to six months. However, it's always good to double-check the specific requirements for your country on the UK government's official website before you go.

For those who do need a visa, the process is straightforward, but you'll want to apply well in advance of your trip. Tourist visas typically allow stays of up to six months, and you'll need to provide documentation, including proof of accommodation and return travel. If you're planning to work or study in Scotland, you'll need to apply for the appropriate visa category, which may have different requirements.

Pro Tip: Make copies of your important documents, including your passport, visa (if required), and any travel confirmations. Keep these copies in a separate location from the originals to ensure you're covered in case anything gets lost.

Currency and Money Matters

The currency used in Scotland is the British Pound Sterling (£), often referred to simply as "the pound." It's important to note that while Scottish banks issue their banknotes, they are interchangeable with other UK banknotes. However, if you plan on travelling to other parts of the UK, such as England or Wales, you may find that some places are unfamiliar with Scottish banknotes and might be hesitant to accept them. It's generally advisable to use up any Scottish notes before leaving the country or simply withdraw cash from ATMs as needed.

Scotland is predominantly a cashless society, so you can use debit and credit cards almost everywhere, from cafes and restaurants to transportation and attractions. Contactless payments are widely accepted, making small purchases quick and easy. However, it's always wise to carry a small amount of cash for rural areas or small vendors who may not accept cards.

Currency Exchange: You can exchange your home currency for pounds at airports, banks, and exchange bureaus, though ATMs typically offer the best exchange rates. Notify your bank of your travel plans to avoid any issues with your cards being blocked for suspicious activity.

Language

The official language in Scotland is English, which is spoken by the vast majority of the population. However, you'll also hear Scots and Scottish Gaelic, especially in certain regions. Scots is a Germanic language closely related to English, and while some words may sound unfamiliar, you'll find that most Scots speakers can easily switch to standard English when needed.

Scottish Gaelic, a Celtic language, is spoken by a small percentage of the population, particularly in the Highlands and the Western Isles. Although you're unlikely to need Gaelic during your trip, you'll see bilingual signs in Gaelic and English, particularly in rural areas. Learning a few phrases can be a fun way to engage with the local culture, even if it's just basic greetings or thank you.

Tip for Travellers: Don't be shy about asking locals to repeat themselves if you don't understand something—Scottish accents can vary significantly across regions, and most people are happy to help!

Health and Safety Tips

Scotland is generally a safe country to visit, with low crime rates and excellent healthcare facilities. However, it's always good to take precautions to ensure your trip goes smoothly.

Healthcare: If you're travelling from within the European Union, you can use your European Health Insurance Card (EHIC) to access necessary medical treatment. However, with Brexit in place, it's wise to check the latest regulations regarding healthcare coverage for EU citizens. Travellers from outside the EU should consider purchasing travel health insurance that covers emergency medical care.

In Scotland, you'll find that healthcare services are of a high standard, with hospitals and clinics well-equipped to handle emergencies. If you need non-emergency medical care, pharmacies (called "chemists" in the UK) can offer advice and over-the-counter medications. Many pharmacies have private consultation rooms where you can discuss health issues in confidence.

Emergency Numbers: The emergency number in Scotland is 999 for police, fire, or ambulance services. If you require non-emergency medical assistance, you can dial 111 for advice and to be directed to the appropriate healthcare service.

Vaccinations: There are no mandatory vaccinations required for Scotland, but it's always wise to ensure that your routine vaccinations, such as those for tetanus, diphtheria, and measles, are up to date. If you're planning outdoor activities in rural areas, consider a tick-borne encephalitis vaccine, as ticks can be an issue in some parts of Scotland.

Staying Safe: While Scotland is a safe destination, it's important to exercise the same caution you would in any other country. Keep your belongings secure, especially in crowded tourist areas, and be mindful of your surroundings, particularly when exploring cities at night. In rural areas, ensure you're prepared for the weather, which can change rapidly—always carry a waterproof jacket and extra layers.

Travel Insurance

Travel insurance is a crucial aspect of trip planning that should never be overlooked. A good travel insurance policy will cover you for a wide range of potential issues, from medical emergencies to trip cancellations, lost luggage, and even missed connections.

Medical Coverage: Ensure your travel insurance includes comprehensive medical coverage, especially if you're engaging in outdoor activities like hiking, skiing, or water sports. Medical expenses can quickly add up, particularly if you require transportation to a hospital or specialized care.

Trip Cancellation and Interruption: Life is unpredictable, and sometimes travel plans change. Look for a policy that offers protection if you need to cancel your trip due to illness, injury, or other unforeseen circumstances. This coverage can also help if your trip is interrupted by weather, natural disasters, or other events beyond your control.

Lost or Stolen Luggage: Travel insurance can also provide compensation for lost, stolen, or delayed luggage. This is particularly important if you're carrying valuable items like electronics, cameras, or even your wardrobe essentials.

Adventure Sports Coverage: If you're planning on partaking in any adventure sports, such as climbing, kayaking, or skiing, make sure your policy covers these activities. Some standard policies may not include high-risk activities, so read the fine print and consider adding extra coverage if needed.

Choosing the Right Policy: When selecting travel insurance, compare different policies and read the terms and conditions carefully. It's important to understand what's covered and what isn't—some policies may exclude certain activities, or pre-existing conditions, or have strict limits on payouts.

Top Tip: Print out a copy of your travel insurance policy and carry it with you. Make sure you have the emergency contact number for your insurance provider easily accessible in case you need to make a claim.

Transportation Options

Scotland is a country with diverse landscapes and vibrant cities, making it a destination that calls for thoughtful travel planning. Whether you're arriving from abroad or navigating the country's charming towns and rugged countryside, understanding your transportation options will help you make the most of your trip. This section provides a comprehensive guide to getting to and around Scotland, covering airports, trains, buses, car rentals, and ferries.

Getting to Scotland

By Air: Airports and Airlines

Scotland is well-connected to the rest of the world by air, with five major airports handling both international and domestic flights. These airports serve as the primary gateways for travellers arriving from various parts of the globe.

Edinburgh Airport (EDI): Located just 8 miles (13 kilometres) west of the city centre, Edinburgh Airport is the busiest airport in Scotland. It handles numerous flights from across Europe, North America, and the

Middle East. Major airlines like British Airways, easyJet, and Ryanair offer regular services. The airport is also well-connected to the city via buses, trams, and taxis.

Glasgow Airport (GLA): Situated about 10 miles (16 kilometres) west of Glasgow's city centre, Glasgow Airport is Scotland's second busiest airport. It offers a wide range of international and domestic flights, with airlines like Emirates, KLM, and Aer Lingus operating from here. The airport is linked to Glasgow by bus, with a direct service running every 10 minutes.

Aberdeen Airport (ABZ): Known as the gateway to the northeast of Scotland and the North Sea oil industry, Aberdeen Airport is located 7 miles (11 kilometres) northwest of the city. It serves flights to destinations across the UK and Europe, with airlines such as British Airways, Flybe, and KLM.

Inverness Airport (INV): This airport, located 8 miles (13 kilometres) northeast of Inverness, is ideal for travellers heading to the Highlands. It offers flights to several UK cities and a few European destinations, with airlines like easyJet and Loganair providing services.

Glasgow Prestwick Airport (PIK): Located 32 miles (51 kilometres) southwest of Glasgow, this smaller airport primarily serves low-cost carriers like Ryanair. It's a convenient entry point for travellers looking for budget flights, especially from Europe.

Travel Tips:

Getting from the Airport: Most Scottish airports are well-served by public transportation, including buses and trains. Taxis and ride-sharing services like Uber are also available but can be more expensive.

Book Early: Scotland is a popular tourist destination, especially during the summer months and festive periods. Book your flights early to secure the best deals and availability.

Connecting Flights: If your destination is in a more remote part of Scotland, you may need to connect through one of the major airports. Domestic flights within Scotland are frequent and relatively quick.

By Train: Rail Links to Scotland

For travellers within the UK, arriving in Scotland by train is a comfortable and scenic option. Scotland's major cities, including Edinburgh, Glasgow, Aberdeen, and Inverness, are well-connected to London and other cities in England by a network of trains.

LNER (London North Eastern Railway): This operator runs regular high-speed services from London King's Cross to Edinburgh, continuing to other Scottish cities like Aberdeen and Inverness. The journey from London to Edinburgh takes around 4.5 hours, making it a convenient option for those who prefer not to fly.

Avanti West Coast: If you're travelling from the west of England, Avanti West Coast offers services from London Euston to Glasgow Central. The journey time is around 4.5 hours, with trains offering comfortable seating, Wi-Fi, and dining options.

Caledonian Sleeper: For a unique experience, the Caledonian Sleeper provides overnight services from London to various destinations in Scotland, including Edinburgh, Glasgow, Inverness, Aberdeen, and Fort William. This train allows you to sleep through the journey and wake up in Scotland, making it both time-efficient and memorable.

Travel Tips:

Booking Tickets: Book your train tickets in advance to get the best prices. Websites like Trainline or the official rail operators' sites offer ticketing options.

Rail Passes: If you plan to travel extensively by train within Scotland, consider purchasing a BritRail pass, which offers unlimited travel for a set number of days.

Enjoy the Scenery: Scotland's rail routes, particularly those in the Highlands, offer stunning views of mountains, lochs, and coastlines. Be sure to grab a window seat!

By Bus: Coach Services to Scotland

Long-distance buses, or coaches, provide another affordable way to travel to Scotland from other parts of the UK. While the journey may take longer than by train, coaches often offer lower fares, making them a popular choice for budget-conscious travellers.

National Express: This coach operator runs services from various UK cities to Scotland, including Edinburgh, Glasgow, Aberdeen, and Inverness. The journey from London to Edinburgh can take around 8-10 hours, depending on traffic and stops.

Megabus: Known for its budget-friendly fares, Megabus offers services from London and other major UK cities to destinations in Scotland. Booking in advance can secure you a seat for as little as a few pounds.

Travel Tips:

Comfort Considerations: While buses are more budget-friendly, they can be less comfortable for long journeys compared to trains. Bring a travel pillow, snacks, and entertainment to make the trip more enjoyable.

Night Buses: If you're short on time, consider taking a night bus to save on both accommodation and travel time.

Getting Around Scotland

Once you've arrived in Scotland, you'll find a range of transportation options to help you explore the country's cities, towns, and countryside. From trains and buses to car rentals and ferries, there's a mode of transport to suit every traveller's needs.

By Train: Scotland's Rail Network

Scotland's rail network is extensive, connecting major cities, towns, and even remote areas. Trains are a convenient way to travel between cities like Edinburgh, Glasgow, Aberdeen, and Inverness, as well as to explore the picturesque Highlands and islands.

ScotRail: The primary train operator within Scotland, ScotRail, runs services across the country. From the scenic West Highland Line, which takes you through breathtaking landscapes, to the East Coast Line connecting Edinburgh and Aberdeen, there's a route for every traveller.

Highland Explorer: This train service is designed for travellers looking to experience the beauty of the Scottish Highlands. It offers panoramic windows and spacious seating, making it perfect for sightseeing.

Borders Railway: If you're interested in exploring the Scottish Borders, this line connects Edinburgh with Tweedbank, passing through charming towns and beautiful countryside.

Travel Tips:

Off-Peak Travel: If you're flexible with your schedule, travelling during off-peak hours can save you money on train fares.

Day Trips: Scotland's compact size means that many destinations are accessible as day trips by train, such as Stirling, St Andrews, and Loch Lomond.

By Bus: Exploring Scotland's Cities and Countryside

Buses are an essential part of Scotland's public transport network, particularly for reaching rural areas not served by trains. You'll find local bus services in cities and towns, as well as long-distance buses that connect different parts of the country.

CityLink: This operator provides long-distance coach services between cities and towns across Scotland, including routes to remote areas like Skye and the Hebrides.

Stagecoach: Stagecoach runs local and regional bus services throughout Scotland, with comprehensive coverage in cities like Aberdeen, Dundee, and Inverness.

Lothian Buses: If you're in Edinburgh, Lothian Buses offers an extensive network of routes across the city and surrounding areas, including a handy airport bus service.

Travel Tips:

Contactless Payment: Many buses in Scotland now accept contactless payment, making it easy to hop on without needing exact change.

Timetables: Bus services in rural areas can be less frequent, so it's a good idea to check timetables in advance, especially if you're planning to return to your accommodation in the evening.

By Car: Renting a Car and Driving in Scotland

Renting a car offers the ultimate flexibility, allowing you to explore Scotland at your own pace. Whether you're planning a road trip through the Highlands or visiting remote castles and villages, having your vehicle can be a great advantage.

Car Rental: Major car rental companies like Avis, Hertz, and Enterprise have branches at airports and in cities across Scotland. Booking in advance is recommended, especially during peak travel seasons.

Driving in Scotland: Scotland's roads vary from modern motorways to narrow, winding country lanes. If you're driving in rural areas, be prepared for single-track roads with passing places. Always keep an eye out for sheep, especially in the Highlands!

Fuel: Petrol stations can be few and far between in remote areas, so fill up when you have the chance. Most stations accept credit and debit cards.

Travel Tips:

Parking: In cities like Edinburgh and Glasgow, parking can be expensive and hard to find. Consider using public transport or park-and-ride facilities when visiting urban areas.

Drive on the Left: Remember that in Scotland, as in the rest of the UK, you drive on the left-hand side of the road.

By Ferry: Reaching the Islands

Scotland's islands are a highlight of any trip, and ferries are the main way to reach many of them. From the Hebrides to Orkney and Shetland, ferry services connect the mainland with Scotland's stunning archipelagos.

Caledonian MacBrayne (CalMac): CalMac operates the majority of ferry services to Scotland's islands, including the Inner and Outer Hebrides.

Ferries depart from various ports along the west coast, including Oban, Mallaig, and Ullapool.

NorthLink Ferries: If you're heading to Orkney or Shetland, NorthLink Ferries offer regular services from Aberdeen, with overnight options available.

Ferry Tips: During peak travel seasons, it's essential to book your ferry tickets in advance, especially if you're bringing a car. Some ferries also offer accommodation for longer journeys, such as the overnight route to Shetland.

Travel Tips:

Weather Considerations: Scotland's weather can be unpredictable, and ferry services may be affected by rough seas. Always check for updates and be prepared for changes to your travel plans.

Island Hopping: If you plan to visit multiple islands, consider purchasing a ferry pass or planning your route carefully to make the most of your time.

Accommodation Guide

Scotland offers a wide range of accommodation options to suit every traveller's needs, from luxurious hotels and historic castles to budget-friendly hostels and cosy bed and breakfasts. Whether you're looking for a high-end retreat in a bustling city, a quaint countryside stay, or a unique experience in a centuries-old castle, Scotland has something to offer. In this section, we'll explore the various types of accommodations available, along with tips to help you choose the right option for your trip.

Luxury Hotels: Indulgence and Comfort

If you're seeking the epitome of comfort and style, Scotland's luxury hotels won't disappoint. From five-star properties in vibrant cities to remote country estates, luxury hotels in Scotland are known for their top-tier service, plush amenities, and breathtaking locations.

City Luxury Hotels: In cities like Edinburgh, Glasgow, and Aberdeen, you'll find a variety of high-end hotels offering everything from contemporary design to historic elegance. Hotels like The Balmoral in Edinburgh, The Principal Blythswood Square in Glasgow, and the Chester Hotel in Aberdeen provide world-class accommodations with luxurious rooms, gourmet dining, and spa facilities.

Country Estates: For a more secluded experience, Scotland's countryside is dotted with luxurious country estates and manor houses. Places like Gleneagles in Perthshire and Inverlochy Castle near Fort William offer the chance to unwind in opulent surroundings while enjoying activities such as golf, falconry, and fine dining.

Boutique Hotels: If you prefer a more intimate experience, Scotland's boutique hotels offer a unique blend of luxury and personal attention. These smaller properties often feature individually designed rooms, personalized service, and a strong connection to local culture. Examples include The Fife Arms in Braemar and The Witchery by the Castle in Edinburgh.

Travel Tips:

Book Early: Scotland's luxury hotels are in high demand, especially during peak travel seasons like summer and the Edinburgh Festival. Booking several months in advance is recommended.

Special Packages: Many luxury hotels offer special packages that include extras like afternoon tea, spa treatments, or guided tours, adding extra value to your stay.

Mid-Range Hotels: Comfort and Convenience

For travellers seeking a balance between comfort and affordability, Scotland's mid-range hotels provide excellent value. These accommodations are typically well-located, offering easy access to popular attractions and amenities without the premium price tag of luxury properties.

Chain Hotels: Well-known hotel chains like Premier Inn, Holiday Inn, and Marriott offer reliable accommodations across Scotland. These hotels are particularly popular in cities and larger towns, where they provide comfortable rooms, on-site dining, and convenient locations near public transport.

Independent Hotels: Many independent hotels in Scotland fall into the mid-range category, offering a more personalized experience without sacrificing comfort. These hotels often reflect the local character and charm, with friendly staff, unique décor, and locally-sourced food. Examples include the Apex Grassmarket Hotel in Edinburgh and the Malmaison in Dundee.

Lodges and Inns: Scotland's countryside and smaller towns are home to charming lodges and inns, which offer a cosy, authentic experience. These accommodations, such as the Clachaig Inn in Glencoe and The Drovers Inn near Loch Lomond, are perfect for travellers looking to explore nature while enjoying hearty Scottish hospitality.

Travel Tips:

Look for Deals: Mid-range hotels often offer deals and discounts, particularly for longer stays or off-peak travel. Websites like Booking.com and Expedia are great for finding special offers.

Location Matters: When choosing a mid-range hotel, consider its proximity to public transport, restaurants, and attractions. Staying slightly outside the city centre can save you money while still providing easy access to everything you want to see.

Budget Hotels and Hostels: Affordable Options for Travellers

Travellers on a budget will find plenty of affordable accommodation options in Scotland, from budget hotel chains to hostels and guesthouses. These options allow you to save money on lodging, freeing up your budget for experiences and activities.

Budget Hotel Chains: For no-frills, reliable accommodations, budget hotel chains like Travelodge and Ibis provide clean, comfortable rooms at affordable prices. These hotels are often located near city centres or major roads, making them convenient for both city breaks and road trips.

Hostels: Scotland has a well-developed network of hostels, catering to budget-conscious travellers, backpackers, and those looking for a social experience. Hostelling Scotland (formerly SYHA) operates many of these properties, offering dormitory-style rooms and private rooms in locations ranging from bustling cities to remote villages. Popular hostels include the Edinburgh Central Youth Hostel and the Skye Basecamp in Broadford.

Guesthouses: Guesthouses, also known as B&Bs (bed and breakfasts), are a popular budget-friendly option in Scotland. These small, family-run establishments offer cosy accommodations, often with a hearty breakfast included. They are widely available across the country, providing a more personal and homely alternative to hotels.

Travel Tips:

Shared Facilities: Hostels often have shared bathrooms and kitchens, so be prepared for a more communal living experience. However, many also offer private rooms if you prefer more privacy.

Membership Discounts: If you're planning to stay in multiple hostels during your trip, consider becoming a member of Hostelling Scotland or other hostel networks to enjoy discounts and benefits.

Unique Stays: Experience Scotland's Heritage and Charm

For travellers seeking something truly special, Scotland offers a range of unique accommodation options that allow you to immerse yourself in the country's history and culture. From staying in a centuries-old castle to a cosy shepherd's hut in the Highlands, these accommodations provide memorable experiences.

Castle Stays: Scotland is famous for its castles, and many of them have been transformed into luxurious hotels or guesthouses. Staying in a castle offers a chance to experience Scotland's rich history firsthand, with many properties featuring original architecture, period furnishings, and even ghost stories. Examples include Dalhousie Castle near Edinburgh, Fonab Castle in Pitlochry, and Inverlochy Castle in the Highlands.

Country Cottages: For a more private and self-sufficient stay, renting a country cottage is a fantastic option. These cottages range from rustic to luxurious and are often located in scenic areas, making them ideal for exploring Scotland's natural beauty. Many cottages come with fully equipped kitchens, cosy fireplaces, and outdoor spaces. Popular locations for cottage rentals include the Isle of Skye, the Cairngorms, and the Scottish Borders.

Shepherd's Huts and Glamping: If you're looking for a unique and eco-friendly stay, consider booking a shepherd's hut, yurt, or glamping pod. These accommodations offer a blend of rustic charm and modern comfort, often set in stunning natural surroundings. Examples include Wigwam Holidays in the Highlands and the luxury glamping site, Loch Ken Eco Bothies, in Dumfries and Galloway.

Converted Churches and Lighthouses: For a truly out-of-the-ordinary experience, Scotland also offers stays in converted churches, lighthouses, and even former schools. These unique properties retain their original character while providing modern amenities. The Lighthouse Keeper's Cottage on the Isle of Mull and the Old Church of Urquhart in Moray are just a couple of examples.

Travel Tips:

Book Early: Unique accommodations tend to be in high demand, especially during peak travel seasons. Booking well in advance is essential to secure your spot.

Check Amenities: While unique stays offer memorable experiences, they may not always have the same level of amenities as hotels. Make sure to check what's included before booking, especially if you have specific needs.

Vacation Rentals: A Home Away from Home

Vacation rentals are an excellent option for travellers seeking the comfort and convenience of a home away from home. From apartments in the heart of Edinburgh to cottages on the Isle of Skye, vacation rentals allow you to live like a local and enjoy more space and flexibility.

City Apartments: If you prefer to stay in the heart of Scotland's cities, vacation rentals like apartments or townhouses offer a more spacious and self-catering option compared to hotels. Many of these properties come with fully equipped kitchens, living areas, and laundry facilities, making them ideal for longer stays. Popular platforms like Airbnb, Vrbo, and Booking.com list a wide range of city apartments in places like Edinburgh, Glasgow, and Inverness.

Countryside Retreats: For a more peaceful escape, countryside vacation rentals provide the perfect base for exploring Scotland's natural beauty. From charming stone cottages to modern eco-lodges, these properties offer privacy and stunning views. The Highlands, the Isle of Skye, and the Cairngorms are particularly popular areas for countryside rentals.

Group Accommodations: If you're travelling with a group or family, vacation rentals offer the added benefit of accommodating larger parties under one roof. Many rentals feature multiple bedrooms and bathrooms, as well as communal spaces for dining and relaxation.

Travel Tips:

Research the Neighborhood: When booking a vacation rental, take the time to research the neighborhood to ensure it's in a convenient location for your activities. Proximity to public transport, grocery stores, and attractions can make a big difference to your stay.

Consider Amenities: Vacation rentals vary widely in terms of amenities, so check the listing carefully to ensure it meets your needs. For example, if you're planning to cook, make sure the kitchen is well-equipped.

Camping and Glamping: Embrace the Great Outdoors

For those who love the outdoors, camping and glamping offer an immersive way to experience Scotland's natural beauty. Whether you prefer traditional camping under the stars or the comfort of a glamping pod, Scotland's diverse landscapes provide the perfect backdrop.

Traditional Camping: Scotland's right to roam laws mean you can wild camp in many areas, allowing you to pitch your tent in remote locations and enjoy the solitude of nature. However, campsites with facilities are also widely available, offering amenities like showers, toilets, and electric hook-ups. Popular camping areas include Loch Lomond, the Cairngorms, and the Isle of Mull.

Glamping: For those who want to enjoy the outdoors without sacrificing comfort, glamping is the perfect compromise. Glamping sites across Scotland offer a range of accommodations, from luxury tents and yurts to eco-friendly pods and cabins. Many glamping sites provide added comforts like real beds, heating, and en-suite bathrooms. Popular glamping locations include the Scottish Borders, the Highlands, and the Isle of Arran.

Travel Tips:

Check Regulations: While wild camping is allowed in many areas, there are restrictions in certain places, such as Loch Lomond and the Trossachs National Park. Always check local regulations before setting up camp.

Be Prepared: Scotland's weather can be unpredictable, so make sure you're prepared for all conditions. Waterproof gear, warm clothing, and a sturdy tent are essential for camping in Scotland.

Packing Tip

Packing for a trip to Scotland can be a bit challenging due to the country's unpredictable weather and diverse range of activities. From hiking in the Highlands to exploring historic cities, you'll need to be prepared for various conditions and experiences. In this section, we'll guide you through the essential items to pack for your Scottish adventure, tailored to the different seasons and activities you might encounter.

Understanding Scotland's Weather

Before diving into the packing list, it's important to understand Scotland's climate. The weather in Scotland can be highly changeable, often experiencing four seasons in a single day. Even in summer, rain showers and cool temperatures are common, while winters can be cold and damp, especially in the northern regions and highlands.

Spring (March to May): Spring in Scotland is mild, with temperatures ranging from 5°C to 15°C (41°F to 59°F). Rain is still a possibility, so packing layers and waterproof gear is essential.

Summer (June to August): Summer is the warmest season, with temperatures typically ranging from 10°C to 20°C (50°F to 68°F). However, rain showers are frequent, and temperatures can drop in the evenings, particularly in the countryside and coastal areas.

Autumn (September to November): Autumn brings cooler temperatures, ranging from 5°C to 15°C (41°F to 59°F), along with stunning foliage and increased rainfall. Layering and waterproof gear are again key.

Winter (December to February): Winters in Scotland can be cold, especially in the Highlands and northern regions, with temperatures ranging from -5°C to 7°C (23°F to 45°F). Snow is possible, particularly in higher elevations, so warm clothing and sturdy footwear are necessary.

Essential Items for All Seasons

Regardless of when you visit Scotland, certain items should always be part of your packing list. These essentials will help you stay comfortable and prepared for Scotland's variable weather conditions.

Waterproof Jacket: A high-quality waterproof jacket is a must for any trip to Scotland. Look for a jacket that is lightweight, breathable, and has a hood to protect you from sudden rain showers.

Comfortable Walking Shoes: Whether you're exploring cities or hiking in the countryside, comfortable walking shoes are essential. Choose shoes that are waterproof, supportive, and suitable for both urban and rural environments.

Layers: Layering is key to adapting to Scotland's changing weather. Pack a mix of lightweight base layers, mid-layers (such as fleece or sweaters), and outer layers that can be easily added or removed as needed.

Daypack: A small, durable daypack is useful for carrying essentials during day trips and excursions. Look for one with waterproofing or a rain cover to protect your belongings.

Travel Umbrella: A compact, wind-resistant travel umbrella can be a lifesaver during unexpected downpours. Even though a waterproof jacket is essential, an umbrella offers extra protection.

Power Adapter: Scotland uses the UK's standard three-pin plug (Type G). If you're travelling from outside the UK, a power adapter will be necessary to charge your devices.

Reusable Water Bottle: Staying hydrated is important, especially if you're planning on doing a lot of walking or hiking. A reusable water bottle is eco-friendly and convenient for refilling throughout the day.

Guidebook or Maps: While smartphones are handy for navigation, having a physical guidebook or map can be helpful, especially in areas with limited mobile service.

Packing for Spring and Autumn

Spring and autumn in Scotland share similar weather patterns, with mild temperatures and a mix of sun and rain. Packing for these seasons requires versatility and preparedness for fluctuating conditions.

Lightweight Base Layers: Start with a moisture-wicking base layer, such as a long-sleeve top or thermal shirt. This will help regulate your body temperature and keep you dry during outdoor activities.

Warm Sweaters or Fleece: Mid-layers like wool sweaters or fleece jackets are essential for staying warm in cooler temperatures. These layers can be easily added or removed as the weather changes.

Waterproof Footwear: In addition to comfortable walking shoes, consider packing waterproof boots, especially if you plan on hiking or spending time in the countryside. Wet, muddy paths are common in spring and autumn.

Scarf, Hat, and Gloves: While these accessories are more commonly associated with winter, Scotland's cool breezes can make them useful in spring and autumn as well, particularly in exposed areas like the coast or highlands.

Jeans or Travel Pants: Sturdy, comfortable pants like jeans or travel pants are ideal for both urban exploration and light outdoor activities. Consider packing quick-dry pants if you expect to encounter a lot of rain.

Packing for Summer

Summer in Scotland may not always bring the warm, sunny weather you'd expect. While you might enjoy some pleasant days, it's essential to be prepared for cooler temperatures and rain showers. Here's what to pack for a Scottish summer:

Shorts and T-Shirts: On warmer days, especially in southern Scotland, you might want to wear shorts and t-shirts. However, make sure to pack layers in case the weather turns.

Lightweight Waterproof Jacket: A lighter waterproof jacket or windbreaker is often sufficient for summer showers. Choose one that's easily packable, so you can carry it with you on day trips.

Sunglasses and Sunscreen: While Scotland isn't known for intense sun, UV rays can still be strong, especially in the summer months. Pack sunglasses and sunscreen to protect your skin and eyes.

Swimwear: If you're planning to visit Scotland's beaches or take a dip in the lochs, bring swimwear. Keep in mind that the water will likely be chilly, even in summer!

Insect Repellent: Scotland's famous midges – tiny, biting insects – can be a nuisance in summer, especially in the Highlands and rural areas. Bring insect repellent to keep them at bay during outdoor activities.

Packing for Winter

Winter in Scotland can be cold and damp, especially in the Highlands and northern regions. Packing the right gear will ensure you stay warm and comfortable, whether you're exploring the cities or heading out into nature.

Thermal Base Layers: Pack thermal tops and bottoms to wear under your clothing. These will provide extra warmth without adding bulk.

Insulated Jacket: A well-insulated, windproof jacket is essential for winter travel in Scotland. Down jackets are a popular choice for their warmth and packability, but make sure yours is water-resistant.

Waterproof Boots: Snow and slush are common in winter, so waterproof boots with good traction are a must. Look for insulated options to keep your feet warm.

Warm Accessories: Pack a thick scarf, hat, and gloves to protect yourself from the cold. Consider gloves that are touchscreen-compatible, so you can use your phone without taking them off.

Wool Socks: Wool socks are excellent for keeping your feet warm and dry during cold weather. They also provide extra cushioning for long walks.

Extra Layers: In addition to your main outerwear, pack extra layers like sweaters, fleece vests, or even a thermal blanket for added warmth during particularly cold days.

Activity-Specific Packing

Your packing list will also vary depending on the activities you plan to do in Scotland. Here are some additional items to consider based on popular activities:

Hiking:

Hiking Boots: If you're planning on tackling Scotland's famous trails, such as the West Highland Way or the Isle of Skye's Quiraing, sturdy hiking boots with ankle support are essential.

Backpack and Hydration System: For longer hikes, bring a daypack with enough space for snacks, a first-aid kit, and extra layers. A hydration bladder or water bottles will help you stay hydrated on the go.

Trekking Poles: Trekking poles can be helpful on uneven terrain, especially in the Highlands.

Wildlife Watching:

Binoculars: If you're interested in birdwatching or spotting wildlife, pack a pair of binoculars for a closer view.

Camera: Bring a camera with a good zoom lens to capture Scotland's wildlife, such as puffins, red deer, and dolphins.

City Exploration:

Comfortable Walking Shoes: While you may already have your main walking shoes packed, consider bringing an extra pair for city exploration.

Foldable Tote Bag: A lightweight, foldable tote bag is handy for carrying souvenirs or shopping finds in cities like Edinburgh and Glasgow.

Cycling:

Cycling Gear: If you're planning to explore Scotland by bike, pack your cycling gear, including a helmet, padded shorts, gloves, and a repair kit.

High-Visibility Clothing: Scotland's weather can change quickly, so high-visibility clothing will help keep you safe on the roads, especially in low-light conditions.

Water Activities:

Wetsuit: If you plan on kayaking, paddleboarding, or surfing, consider bringing a wetsuit, as the water can be cold even in summer.

Dry Bag: A dry bag will protect your belongings from getting wet during water-based activities.

Final Packing Tips

Travel-Sized Toiletries: Pack travel-sized toiletries to save space in your luggage. Many accommodations in Scotland provide basic toiletries, so you may not need to bring large bottles.

Laundry Essentials: If you're travelling for an extended period, consider packing a small bottle of travel detergent and a portable clothesline. This will allow you to do laundry on the go and minimize the amount of clothing you need to pack.

Luggage Options: Depending on your travel style, choose between a suitcase or a backpack. If you plan on moving between multiple destinations, a backpack may be more practical. For those staying in one location, a suitcase with wheels could be more convenient.

Budgeting Your Trip

When planning a trip to Scotland, budgeting is a crucial step to ensure you get the most out of your experience without overspending. Scotland offers a wide range of travel experiences, from luxury to budget-friendly, and understanding the average costs for accommodation, food, transportation, and activities will help you allocate your funds wisely. This section will guide you through budgeting for your trip, offering tips and insights on what to expect in terms of expenses.

Understanding the Cost of Travelling in Scotland

Scotland is often perceived as an expensive destination, but with careful planning, it's possible to enjoy everything the country has to offer without breaking the bank. Costs can vary greatly depending on your travel style, the time of year, and the locations you visit. Cities like Edinburgh and Glasgow tend to be more expensive, especially during peak tourist seasons, while rural areas and smaller towns can offer more affordable options.

Here's a breakdown of what you can expect to spend on the major aspects of your trip:

Accommodation Costs

Accommodation in Scotland ranges from budget hostels to luxurious hotels and unique stays like castles and bed & breakfasts. Prices can vary significantly based on location, season, and type of accommodation.

Budget Accommodation (Hostels, Budget Hotels, B&Bs):

Hostels: If you're travelling on a tight budget, hostels are a great option. Dormitory beds typically cost between £15-£30 per night. Some hostels also offer private rooms at a higher cost, around £40-£70 per night.

Budget Hotels: Budget hotels and B&Bs generally range from £50-£100 per night for a double room. These are ideal for travellers who want a bit more privacy and comfort without spending too much.

Guesthouses and B&Bs: These offer a cosy and authentic Scottish experience, with prices ranging from £60-£120 per night depending on the location and level of comfort.

Mid-Range Accommodation (3-4 Star Hotels, Self-Catering Apartments):

Hotels: Mid-range hotels typically cost between £80-£150 per night for a double room. In cities like Edinburgh or Glasgow, expect to pay at the higher end of that range, especially during peak tourist seasons.

Self-Catering Apartments: Renting an apartment or holiday home can be a cost-effective option, especially if you're travelling with a group. Prices vary widely depending on the size and location, but you can expect to pay around £100-£200 per night.

Luxury Accommodation (5-Star Hotels, Castles, Boutique Hotels):

Luxury Hotels: If you're looking to splurge, Scotland offers some fantastic luxury accommodations. Prices for 5-star hotels and boutique stays can range from £200-£500+ per night. Staying in a castle or historic estate often falls into this category, providing a unique and memorable experience.

Unique Stays: Staying in a Scottish castle, a cosy countryside cottage, or a remote bothy can be an unforgettable experience. Prices vary widely, with some castles offering rooms starting at £150 per night, while more exclusive stays can exceed £1,000 per night.

Budget Tip: To save on accommodation, consider travelling during the off-peak season (late autumn to early spring). Prices tend to drop outside of the busy summer months and major festivals like the Edinburgh Fringe.

Food and Drink Costs

Scotland has a rich culinary scene, from hearty traditional fare to modern fine dining. Depending on your preferences and budget, food costs can range from inexpensive street eats to high-end restaurants.

Budget Dining:

Fast Food and Street Food: A meal from a fast food outlet or street food vendor typically costs between £5-£10. In cities, you'll find a variety of affordable options, from fish and chips to international cuisine.

Cafés and Pubs: For a budget-friendly meal, head to a local café or pub. Traditional dishes like haggis, neeps, and tatties can cost around £8-£15. Pubs often offer set menus or daily specials that provide good value for money.

Mid-Range Dining:

Casual Restaurants: In a mid-range restaurant, you can expect to pay around £15-£25 for a main course. Many restaurants offer fixed-price menus, which can be a great way to enjoy a three-course meal for a reasonable price, usually around £20-£30.

Traditional Scottish Restaurants: For an authentic taste of Scotland, dining at a traditional Scottish restaurant is a must. A full meal with a starter, main, and dessert typically costs around £30-£50 per person.

High-End Dining:

Fine Dining: Scotland is home to several Michelin-starred restaurants, where you can indulge in gourmet cuisine. Expect to pay £50-£100+ per person for a tasting menu or a multi-course meal.

Whisky and Dining Experiences: Whisky is a big part of Scottish culture, and many high-end restaurants offer whisky-pairing menus. These experiences can range from £70-£150 per person, depending on the selection and venue.

Budget Tip: If you're staying in self-catering accommodation, shopping at local markets and preparing your own meals can significantly reduce your food costs. Many supermarkets in Scotland offer affordable, high-quality produce, and ready-made meals.

Transportation Costs

Getting around Scotland can be one of the more expensive aspects of your trip, particularly if you're travelling long distances or opting for private transport. However, there are several options to suit different budgets.

Public Transportation:

Buses: Buses are the most affordable way to travel within cities and between towns. A single ticket on a city bus typically costs £1.50-£3, while longer intercity journeys can range from £10-£30 depending on the distance.

Trains: Train travel in Scotland is comfortable and efficient, but it can be pricey if booked last minute. A one-way ticket between major cities like Edinburgh and Glasgow costs around £10-£20. For longer journeys, such as Edinburgh to Inverness, expect to pay £30-£60. Booking in advance or using a rail pass can help reduce costs.

Tram: Edinburgh has a tram service that connects the city centre with the airport and other key areas. Tickets range from £1.70 for a single journey within the city to £6 for airport transfers.

Car Rentals:

Renting a car gives you the freedom to explore Scotland at your own pace, especially in rural areas where public transport may be limited. Car rental costs vary depending on the type of vehicle and the rental duration. On average, expect to pay £25-£50 per day for a standard car, plus fuel costs.

Fuel Prices: Fuel in Scotland is relatively expensive, with petrol prices averaging around £1.45-£1.60 per liter. If you're planning a road trip, factor in fuel costs, as they can add up quickly, especially in remote areas where fuel stations are scarce.

Taxis and Ride-Sharing:

Taxis in Scotland are generally more expensive than public transport, with fares starting at around £3-£5 for short journeys and increasing based on distance and time of day. Ride-sharing services like Uber are available in major cities and can be more cost-effective than traditional taxis.

Airport Transfers: If you're arriving in Scotland by air, consider the cost of airport transfers. A taxi from Edinburgh Airport to the city centre costs around £20-£30, while Glasgow Airport transfers are similar.

Ferries:

If you're planning to visit Scotland's islands, such as the Isle of Skye or the Outer Hebrides, you'll need to budget for ferry travel. Prices vary depending on the route and the size of your vehicle, but a passenger ticket typically costs between £5-£20. If you're bringing a car, expect to pay around £30-£50 for a one-way journey.

Budget Tip: If you plan to use public transportation frequently, consider purchasing a travel pass or card, such as the ScotRail Pass or a city-specific transport card. These passes can offer significant savings compared to buying individual tickets.

Activity and Sightseeing Costs

Scotland is rich in history, culture, and natural beauty, with plenty of activities and attractions to suit every interest and budget. While some experiences can be costly, there are also many free or low-cost options available.

Free Activities:

Museums and Galleries: Many of Scotland's top museums and galleries, including the National Museum of Scotland in Edinburgh and the Kelvingrove Art Gallery and Museum in Glasgow, offer free admission. These cultural institutions provide fascinating insights into Scotland's history, art, and heritage without any cost.

Outdoor Activities: Exploring Scotland's stunning landscapes is often free. Hiking, walking, and enjoying the country's national parks, such as the Cairngorms and Loch Lomond, are great ways to experience Scotland's natural beauty without spending much money.

Paid Activities:

Castles and Historic Sites: Scotland is famous for its castles, and many charge admission fees. Popular sites like Edinburgh Castle, Stirling Castle, and Urquhart Castle typically charge £10-£20 for entry. Consider purchasing a Historic Scotland Explorer Pass, which provides access to multiple sites at a discounted rate.

Guided Tours: Guided tours, such as city walking tours, whisky distillery tours, and boat tours, can add to your overall costs. Prices for guided tours range from £15-£50 per person, depending on the experience and duration.

Outdoor Adventures: If you're interested in outdoor activities like kayaking, cycling, or wildlife watching, expect to pay around £20-£50 for rentals or guided experiences.

Budget Tip: To save on attractions, consider purchasing a sightseeing pass, such as the Edinburgh City Pass or the Scotland Explorer Pass. These passes offer discounted or free entry to multiple attractions, making them a good value if you plan on visiting several paid sites.

Miscellaneous Expenses

Don't forget to budget for miscellaneous expenses such as travel insurance, souvenirs, and tips.

Travel Insurance: Travel insurance is essential for covering unexpected costs such as medical emergencies, trip cancellations, or lost luggage. Prices vary depending on the coverage, but expect to pay around £20-£50 for a standard policy.

Souvenirs and Shopping: Scotland is known for its high-quality goods, from tartan and whisky to handmade crafts. If you plan on shopping for souvenirs, set aside a budget of £50-£200, depending on what you're looking to buy.

Tipping: Tipping is not mandatory in Scotland, but it's appreciated for good service. In restaurants, it's customary to leave a tip of around 10-15% of the bill. For taxis and hotel staff, rounding up the fare or leaving a small tip is standard practice.

Budgeting Tips for Scotland

Plan Ahead: Research and book your accommodation, transportation, and activities in advance to secure the best prices.

Travel Off-Peak: Consider travelling during the shoulder or off-peak seasons to take advantage of lower prices on accommodation and flights.

Use Discounts: Look for discounts, deals, and passes that can help you save money on attractions, transportation, and dining.

Track Your Spending: Keep a daily budget and track your expenses to avoid overspending. This will help you stay within your budget and make adjustments as needed.

CHAPTER 3

TOP DESTINATIONS IN SCOTLAND

Edinburgh

Edinburgh, the capital of Scotland, is a city steeped in history, culture, and natural beauty. Nestled between the Firth of Forth and a range of hills, Edinburgh's striking skyline is a blend of medieval structures, Georgian architecture, and modern design. This chapter delves into the heart of the city, offering an in-depth guide to its most iconic attractions, as well as the hidden gems that make Edinburgh one of the most beloved cities in the world.

Edinburgh Castle: The Crown Jewel of the City

Perched atop Castle Rock, a volcanic outcrop, Edinburgh Castle dominates the city's skyline. The castle's history dates back to the 12th century, and it has served as a royal residence, military stronghold, and now, as one of Scotland's most popular tourist attractions.

What to See Inside the Castle:

The Crown Jewels and the Stone of Destiny: Housed in the Crown Room, the Crown Jewels of Scotland, also known as the Honours of Scotland, are among the oldest in Europe. The Stone of Destiny, a symbol of Scottish royalty, was returned to Scotland in 1996 and is displayed alongside the jewels. This sacred stone has been used in the coronation of Scottish kings for centuries, and its presence in the castle adds a layer of mystique to the visit.

The Great Hall: Constructed during the reign of King James IV, the Great Hall is a magnificent example of medieval architecture. The hall's vaulted ceiling and stained-glass windows transport visitors back to the days of grand banquets and royal ceremonies. Today, the hall houses a collection of weapons and armour, offering a glimpse into Scotland's martial past.

St. Margaret's Chapel: This small yet significant chapel is the oldest surviving building in Edinburgh, dating back to the early 12th century.

Dedicated to Queen Margaret, who was canonized in 1250, the chapel is a place of quiet reflection amidst the bustle of the castle.

The National War Museum: Located within the castle, this museum provides an extensive overview of Scotland's military history. Exhibits include everything from uniforms and medals to paintings and personal letters, offering a poignant insight into the lives of Scottish soldiers.

The Castle's Strategic Importance:

Edinburgh Castle's strategic position has made it a focal point in Scotland's history. It has withstood numerous sieges and has played a key role in many conflicts, including the Wars of Scottish Independence. The views from the castle's battlements are unparalleled, providing a panoramic vista of the city, the surrounding countryside, and the distant Highlands.

Special Events:

One of the highlights of Edinburgh Castle is the daily firing of the One O'Clock Gun, a tradition that dates back to 1861. Originally intended as a time signal for ships in the Firth of Forth, it remains a popular attraction for visitors. During the summer months, the castle also hosts the Royal Edinburgh Military Tattoo, a spectacular display of military bands, dancers, and performers from around the world, set against the backdrop of the illuminated castle.

The Royal Mile: Edinburgh's Historic Heart

Stretching from Edinburgh Castle to the Palace of Holyroodhouse, the Royal Mile is a historic thoroughfare that forms the backbone of the city's Old Town. Lined with ancient buildings, hidden courtyards, and cobblestone streets, the Royal Mile is a journey through Edinburgh's rich past.

Top Attractions Along the Royal Mile:

St. Giles' Cathedral: Often referred to as the High Kirk of Edinburgh, St. Giles' Cathedral is the focal point of the Scottish Reformation. Its distinctive crown steeple has become a symbol of the city. Inside, visitors can admire the stunning stained glass windows, intricate carvings, and the Thistle Chapel, which is dedicated to the Order of the Thistle, Scotland's highest chivalric order.

The Real Mary King's Close: Beneath the bustling streets of the Royal Mile lies a hidden world of underground alleys and chambers. The Real Mary King's Close offers guided tours that explore these forgotten streets, providing a glimpse into the lives of the people who lived there during the 17th century. The close is named after Mary King, a merchant who lived and worked on the close in the 1630s. The tour is both fascinating and eerie, revealing the darker side of Edinburgh's history.

The Scottish Parliament: At the foot of the Royal Mile, the Scottish Parliament is a striking example of modern architecture. Designed by Enric Miralles, the building reflects Scotland's landscape and heritage. Visitors can take guided tours of the parliament, learning about its role in contemporary Scottish politics and the building's unique design elements.

Holyrood Palace: The official residence of the British monarch in Scotland, Holyrood Palace is steeped in history. The palace has witnessed many key events in Scottish history, including the life of Mary, Queen of Scots. Visitors can explore the state apartments, the Great Gallery, and the ruins of Holyrood Abbey. The palace gardens, with their lush lawns and flowerbeds, offer a peaceful retreat from the city's hustle and bustle.

Hidden Gems on the Royal Mile:

While the main attractions draw the crowds, the Royal Mile is also home to several lesser-known spots that are well worth a visit:

The Writers' Museum: Tucked away in Lady Stair's Close, the Writers' Museum celebrates the lives and works of Scotland's literary giants— Robert Burns, Sir Walter Scott, and Robert Louis Stevenson. The museum's collection includes rare books, manuscripts, portraits, and personal items, offering a unique insight into the minds of these iconic authors.

Gladstone's Land: This 17th-century tenement house offers a glimpse into the lives of Edinburgh's residents during the 1600s. Restored by the National Trust for Scotland, the house features period furnishings, painted ceilings, and a shopfront that reflects the building's mercantile past.

Museum of Edinburgh: Located in the Canongate area of the Royal Mile, the Museum of Edinburgh tells the story of the city through a collection of artefacts, paintings, and memorabilia. The museum's exhibits cover everything from the city's medieval origins to its role in the Enlightenment and beyond.

Arthur's Seat: The Best View in Edinburgh

For those who love the outdoors, a hike up Arthur's Seat is an absolute must. This ancient volcanic hill, which rises 251 meters above sea level, offers breathtaking views of the city and the surrounding landscape. Despite its elevation, Arthur's Seat is easily accessible from the city centre, making it a popular spot for both locals and tourists.

The Legend of Arthur's Seat:

Arthur's Seat is steeped in myth and legend. Some believe that the hill is the site of the legendary Camelot, while others suggest it may have been named after a local king. The hill's mysterious atmosphere is enhanced by its geological formations, which have inspired countless stories over the centuries.

Hiking Routes:

There are several routes to the summit of Arthur's Seat, catering to different levels of fitness and experience. The most popular path starts from the east side of Holyrood Park, near Dunsapie Loch. This route is relatively gentle, with a gradual incline leading to the summit. For a more challenging hike, the route from the west side of the park offers steeper climbs and rugged terrain.

What to Expect at the Summit:

Reaching the top of Arthur's Seat is a rewarding experience. On a clear day, the views stretch as far as the Firth of Forth, the Pentland Hills, and even the Highlands. The summit also offers a unique perspective of Edinburgh, with its blend of medieval and modern architecture laid out below. The experience of standing atop Arthur's Seat, with the wind in your hair and the city at your feet, stays with you long after you leave Edinburgh.

Holyrood Park:

Arthur's Seat is part of Holyrood Park, a sprawling green space that offers a variety of outdoor activities. The park's diverse landscape includes cliffs, lochs, and rugged crags, making it a haven for nature lovers. In addition to hiking, visitors can enjoy birdwatching, picnicking, and exploring the park's historical sites, such as St. Anthony's Chapel, a 15th-century ruin with stunning views over the city.

Glasgow

Glasgow, Scotland's largest city, is a dynamic and diverse destination known for its vibrant arts scene, exceptional shopping, and lively nightlife. Often considered the cultural heart of Scotland, Glasgow is a city that has undergone significant transformation over the years. From its industrial roots to its present-day status as a bustling hub of creativity and entertainment, Glasgow offers an eclectic mix of experiences that cater to every type of traveller. This chapter provides an in-depth exploration of the city, highlighting its most notable attractions and the unique character that makes Glasgow a must-visit destination.

The Arts and Culture of Glasgow: A Creative Powerhouse

Glasgow's reputation as a cultural capital is well-deserved, with a rich history of artistic innovation and a thriving contemporary art scene. The city is home to some of the most renowned museums, galleries, and performance spaces in the UK, making it a paradise for art lovers and culture enthusiasts.

Kelvingrove Art Gallery and Museum:

One of Glasgow's most iconic landmarks, the Kelvingrove Art Gallery and Museum is a must-visit for anyone interested in art, history, and culture. Housed in a stunning red sandstone building in the West End of the city, the museum features 22 galleries showcasing everything from Renaissance art to natural history.

Art Collections: The Kelvingrove's art collection is one of the finest in Europe, with works by famous artists such as Rembrandt, Van Gogh, and Salvador Dalí. The museum is also home to the celebrated painting "Christ of Saint John of the Cross" by Dalí, which draws art lovers from around the world.

Natural History Exhibits: The museum's natural history exhibits are equally impressive, featuring everything from dinosaur skeletons to a taxidermy display of Sir Roger, the beloved Asian elephant that once lived at the Glasgow Zoo.

Interactive Displays: Kelvingrove is known for its family-friendly approach, with interactive displays and hands-on exhibits that make learning fun for visitors of all ages. The museum's diverse collections ensure that there is something for everyone, whether you're an art aficionado or a history buff.

The Glasgow School of Art:

Founded in 1845, the Glasgow School of Art (GSA) is one of the leading art schools in the world and a symbol of the city's artistic heritage. The school's main building, designed by the renowned architect Charles Rennie Mackintosh, is considered a masterpiece of Art Nouveau architecture. Although the building suffered significant damage in two fires (in 2014 and 2018), efforts are ongoing to restore this architectural gem to its former glory.

Mackintosh's Legacy: Charles Rennie Mackintosh's influence extends beyond the GSA, with several of his architectural works scattered throughout the city. Fans of his work can explore the Mackintosh House at the University of Glasgow, which has been meticulously reconstructed to reflect the original interiors designed by Mackintosh.

Contemporary Art Scene: The GSA has produced many influential artists, including several Turner Prize winners. Today, Glasgow's contemporary art scene continues to thrive, with numerous galleries and artist-run spaces showcasing cutting-edge works. The Centre for Contemporary Arts (CCA) and the Tramway are two of the city's leading venues for contemporary art exhibitions and performances.

Theatre and Performance:

Glasgow is also a city of theatre, with a vibrant performance scene that caters to a wide range of tastes. From classic productions to experimental performances, Glasgow's theatres offer something for everyone.

Theatre Royal: The Theatre Royal is Glasgow's oldest theatre, dating back to 1867. It is home to Scottish Opera and Scottish Ballet, two of the country's premier performing arts companies. The theatre's elegant interior and historic charm make it a favourite venue for opera, ballet, and drama.

The King's Theatre: Another historic venue, the King's Theatre, is known for hosting touring West End productions, as well as pantomimes and musical performances. Its grand architecture and central location make it a popular choice for an evening out in Glasgow.

The Tron Theatre: For those interested in contemporary theatre, the Tron Theatre offers an exciting program of new works and experimental productions. Located in the Merchant City area, the Tron is known for its intimate atmosphere and commitment to nurturing emerging talent.

Shopping in Glasgow: A Retail Paradise

Glasgow is often hailed as the best shopping destination in the UK outside of London, and it's easy to see why. The city offers a mix of high-end fashion, independent boutiques, vintage shops, and bustling markets, ensuring that every shopper can find something to suit their taste and budget.

Buchanan Street: The Style Mile

At the heart of Glasgow's shopping district lies Buchanan Street, a pedestrianized thoroughfare known as the "Style Mile." This bustling street is lined with flagship stores, designer boutiques, and high-street favourites, making it the go-to destination for fashion enthusiasts.

Princes Square: For a more upscale shopping experience, head to Princes Square, an elegant shopping centre housed in a beautifully restored

Victorian building. With its luxurious boutiques, stylish cafes, and striking interior design, Princes Square is a destination in itself.

The Buchanan Galleries: Another major shopping destination on Buchanan Street, the Buchanan Galleries is a large mall that offers a wide range of retailers, from high-street brands to department stores. It's the perfect place to shop for everything from clothing and accessories to homeware and electronics.

The Merchant City: Chic and Unique

The Merchant City area of Glasgow is known for its trendy boutiques, independent stores, and chic cafes. This stylish district is a haven for those looking to discover unique fashion pieces, artisanal goods, and quirky home decor.

Vintage and Second-Hand Shops: Glasgow has a thriving vintage scene, with several shops in the Merchant City offering an eclectic mix of retro clothing, accessories, and homeware. Whether you're looking for a 1950s cocktail dress or a rare vinyl record, you're sure to find something special.

The Barras Market: For a truly Glaswegian shopping experience, visit The Barras Market in the East End of the city. This iconic market has been a fixture in Glasgow since the 1920s, offering everything from antiques and collectables to fresh produce and street food. The market's lively atmosphere and colourful characters make it a must-visit for anyone looking to experience the local culture.

West End Wonders: Byres Road and Beyond

The West End of Glasgow is another great shopping destination, with Byres Road at its heart. This bustling street is lined with independent boutiques, bookstores, and quirky gift shops, making it the perfect place to find a unique souvenir or gift.

Ashton Lane: Just off Byres Road, Ashton Lane is a cobbled alleyway known for its charming cafes, bars, and boutiques. The Lane's twinkling fairy lights and bohemian vibe make it a favourite spot for both locals and visitors.

De Courcy's Arcade: Tucked away in the West End, De Courcy's Arcade is a hidden gem that houses a collection of independent shops and studios. From handmade jewellery to vintage furniture, this quirky arcade is full of surprises.

Glasgow's Nightlife: A City That Never Sleeps

When the sun sets, Glasgow comes alive with a vibrant nightlife that caters to every taste and style. Whether you're looking for a cosy pub, a trendy cocktail bar, or a lively nightclub, Glasgow has it all.

Traditional Pubs and Live Music:

Glasgow's pub scene is legendary, with a wide variety of establishments offering everything from craft beers to traditional ales. Many of the city's pubs also host live music, making them the perfect place to enjoy a pint while listening to local bands.

The Clutha: A Glasgow institution, The Clutha is a historic pub that has been serving up drinks and live music since the 19th century. The pub's walls are adorned with murals of famous Glaswegians, and its lively atmosphere makes it a favourite with both locals and tourists.

King Tut's Wah Wah Hut: If you're a fan of live music, King Tut's is a must-visit. This iconic venue is known for hosting up-and-coming bands, and many famous acts, including Oasis and Radiohead, have played here early in their careers. The intimate setting and legendary reputation make it one of the best places in Glasgow to catch a gig.

Trendy Bars and Cocktails:

For those who prefer a more sophisticated night out, Glasgow's bar scene offers plenty of stylish spots to sip on a cocktail or two. From speakeasy-style bars to rooftop terraces, there's something for everyone.

The Finnieston: Located in the trendy Finnieston area, this bar is known for its expertly crafted cocktails and nautical-themed decor. The Finnieston specializes in gin, with an impressive selection of Scottish gins on offer. The bar's relaxed yet stylish atmosphere makes it a great place to start your evening.

The Ivy Buchanan Street: For a touch of glamour, head to The Ivy on Buchanan Street. This chic brasserie and bar offers an extensive cocktail menu in a luxurious setting. Whether you're enjoying a pre-dinner drink or a nightcap, The Ivy's sophisticated ambience is sure to impress.

Nightclubs and Late-Night Entertainment:

Glasgow's nightlife wouldn't be complete without its legendary clubs, which keep the party going until the early hours. Whether you're into electronic music, indie rock, or hip-hop, Glasgow's clubs offer a night out to remember.

Sub Club: One of the oldest and most famous nightclubs in the world, Sub Club is a must-visit for fans of electronic music. Known for its incredible sound system and top-notch DJs, Sub Club has been a staple of Glasgow's nightlife since 1987.

SWG3: Located in a former warehouse in the West End, SWG3 is a multi-arts venue that hosts everything from club nights to art exhibitions. With its industrial-chic vibe and eclectic lineup of events, SWG3 is one of the coolest spots in the city for a night out.

The Highlands

The Scottish Highlands are a region of unparalleled natural beauty, where rugged mountains, deep lochs, and vast glens create a landscape that is both awe-inspiring and steeped in history. Covering much of the northern part of Scotland, the Highlands offer some of the most scenic and unspoiled areas in the country, making it a must-visit destination for nature lovers, outdoor enthusiasts, and anyone seeking a deeper connection with Scotland's wild and mystical past. This chapter provides a comprehensive guide to exploring the Highlands, focusing on iconic landmarks such as Loch Ness, Ben Nevis, and Glen Coe, and offering insights into the unique charm and character of this extraordinary region.

Loch Ness: The Legendary Loch

Loch Ness is arguably the most famous body of water in Scotland, known worldwide for its mysterious resident, the Loch Ness Monster, affectionately referred to as "Nessie." However, there is much more to Loch Ness than tales of a mythical creature. This vast freshwater loch, stretching for over 23 miles, is surrounded by stunning scenery and offers a variety of activities and attractions for visitors.

Exploring the Loch:

Loch Ness is the second-largest loch by surface area in Scotland but is the largest by volume, holding more water than all the lakes in England and Wales combined. The loch's dark, peaty waters, and the dramatic hills that rise steeply from its shores, create a sense of mystery and wonder that captivates all who visit.

Cruises on the Loch: One of the best ways to experience Loch Ness is by taking a boat cruise. Several companies offer guided tours of the loch, providing an opportunity to enjoy the stunning scenery while learning about the history, geology, and, of course, the legends associated with the loch. Some cruises even include sonar equipment, allowing you to search for signs of Nessie as you glide across the water.

Urquhart Castle: Perched on the western shore of Loch Ness, Urquhart Castle is a historic fortress that dates back to the 13th century. The castle ruins, set against the backdrop of the loch and the surrounding hills, offer one of the most iconic views in Scotland. Visitors can explore the castle grounds, learn about its turbulent history, and enjoy panoramic views from the Grant Tower, the highest point of the castle.

Loch Ness Centre & Exhibition: Located in the village of Drumnadrochit, the Loch Ness Centre & Exhibition provides an in-depth look at the natural and cultural history of Loch Ness, as well as the enduring legend of the Loch Ness Monster. Through a series of exhibits and interactive displays, visitors can explore the scientific explanations for the sightings and the cultural impact of Nessie on Scotland and the world.

Outdoor Activities Around Loch Ness:

Beyond the loch itself, the surrounding area offers a wealth of outdoor activities that make the most of the Highland landscape.

Hiking and Walking: The Great Glen Way, a long-distance trail that stretches from Fort William to Inverness, passes along the western shore of Loch Ness. This scenic route offers a variety of walking options, from short strolls to multi-day hikes, allowing you to experience the beauty of the loch and the surrounding countryside. For those looking for a shorter walk, the South Loch Ness Trail offers stunning views and the chance to explore hidden gems along the quieter southern shore.

Cycling: The area around Loch Ness is also popular with cyclists, with several well-marked routes that cater to all levels of experience. The Caledonia Way, part of the National Cycle Network, runs along the loch's eastern shore and offers a challenging but rewarding ride through some of Scotland's most spectacular landscapes.

Ben Nevis: Conquering Scotland's Highest Peak

Rising to a height of 1,345 meters (4,413 feet), Ben Nevis is the tallest mountain in the British Isles and a magnet for climbers, hikers, and outdoor enthusiasts. Located near the town of Fort William, often referred to as the "Outdoor Capital of the UK," Ben Nevis offers a range of experiences, from challenging ascents to breathtaking views.

Climbing Ben Nevis:

For many, reaching the summit of Ben Nevis is the ultimate goal, and the mountain attracts thousands of climbers each year. The most popular route to the top is the Mountain Track (often referred to as the Tourist Path or Pony Track), which starts at the Glen Nevis Visitor Centre and follows a well-trodden path to the summit.

The Ascent: While the Mountain Track is the most straightforward route, it is still a demanding hike, requiring a good level of fitness and preparation. The ascent takes approximately 4-5 hours, with the descent taking a further 2-3 hours. Along the way, hikers will pass through a range of environments, from grassy lower slopes to rocky and barren upper reaches. The summit is often covered in snow, even in summer, and offers panoramic views of the surrounding Highlands on clear days.

Safety Considerations: Given the unpredictable weather in the Highlands, climbers should be well-prepared for all conditions. Proper clothing, equipment, and navigation tools are essential, as the weather can change rapidly, and the path can be challenging to follow in poor visibility. For those less experienced or unsure of their abilities, guided walks are available, offering the expertise of local guides who are familiar with the mountain and its conditions.

Exploring the Nevis Range:

Even if you're not planning to summit Ben Nevis, the surrounding Nevis Range offers plenty of opportunities to enjoy the beauty and adventure of the Highlands.

Nevis Range Mountain Resort: Located near Fort William, the Nevis Range Mountain Resort is a popular destination for outdoor activities year-round. In the winter, the resort offers skiing and snowboarding, while in the summer, it becomes a haven for mountain bikers, climbers, and hikers. The resort's gondola provides an easy way to access the mountain, offering stunning views and access to a network of trails.

Glen Nevis: The glen that lies at the foot of Ben Nevis is a stunning area of natural beauty, with lush forests, sparkling streams, and dramatic waterfalls. The Steall Falls, one of the highest waterfalls in Scotland, is a highlight of the glen and can be reached via a scenic walk through the Nevis Gorge. The area is also rich in wildlife, and it's not uncommon to spot red deer, golden eagles, and other native species.

Glen Coe: Scotland's Most Scenic Valley

Glen Coe, often described as Scotland's most beautiful and dramatic glen, is a place of stark contrasts, where towering mountains and deep valleys create a landscape that is both breathtaking and haunting. The glen, located in the Lochaber area of the Highlands, is steeped in history and has become one of the most iconic symbols of Scotland's wild and rugged beauty.

The History of Glen Coe:

Glen Coe is perhaps best known for the tragic events of the Massacre of Glen Coe, which took place in 1692. The massacre, in which members of the Clan MacDonald were killed by government forces, has left an indelible mark on the history and culture of the area. Visitors to the glen can learn more about this dark chapter at the Glen Coe Visitor Centre, which provides historical context and explores the broader story of the Highlands during this tumultuous period.

Hiking and Exploring Glen Coe:

Glen Coe is a paradise for hikers, with a range of trails that offer everything from gentle walks to challenging scrambles. The dramatic scenery, with its steep-sided mountains and sweeping views, makes every step a memorable experience.

The Three Sisters: One of the most iconic views in Glen Coe is that of the Three Sisters, a trio of ridges that rise majestically from the valley floor. The area around the Three Sisters offers several hiking routes, including the popular walk to the Lost Valley (Coire Gabhail), a hidden glen that was historically used by the MacDonalds to hide their cattle.

The Aonach Eagach Ridge: For experienced hikers and climbers, the Aonach Eagach Ridge is one of the most challenging and exhilarating routes in Scotland. This narrow ridge runs along the northern side of Glen Coe and offers a thrilling scramble with breathtaking views. The ridge is not for the faint-hearted and should only be attempted by those with experience in scrambling and a good head for heights.

Glen Etive: A short drive from Glen Coe, Glen Etive is another stunning valley that offers a more peaceful and remote experience. The glen is famous for its role in the James Bond film "Skyfall," and its serene beauty has made it a favourite spot for photographers, hikers, and those looking to escape the crowds.

Wildlife and Nature in Glen Coe:

The natural beauty of Glen Coe is complemented by its rich wildlife, with the area being home to a variety of species that thrive in the Highland environment.

Red Deer: The sight of red deer grazing in the glen is a common one, particularly in the early morning or late evening. These majestic animals are a symbol of the Scottish Highlands, and their presence adds to the wild and untamed feel of the landscape.

Golden Eagles: Glen Coe is also a prime location for spotting golden eagles, one of Scotland's most iconic birds of prey. These magnificent birds can often be seen soaring high above the glen, their keen eyesight scanning the terrain for prey.

Flora: The glen's diverse habitats support a wide range of plant life, from the heather-covered moorlands to the ancient woodlands that cling to the lower slopes. In the spring and summer, the glen comes alive with the colours of wildflowers, adding to the beauty of the landscape.

Isle of Skye

The Isle of Skye, often referred to as the "Misty Isle," is one of Scotland's most iconic and enchanting destinations. Known for its dramatic landscapes, picturesque villages, and rich cultural heritage, Skye has captured the hearts of travellers for centuries. Whether you are drawn by the island's rugged cliffs, serene lochs, or the mystical allure of its folklore, a visit to the Isle of Skye is an experience that lingers long after you leave. This chapter offers an in-depth exploration of the Isle of Skye, guiding you through its breathtaking natural wonders, charming towns, and unique attractions that make it a must-visit destination in Scotland.

Introduction to the Isle of Skye

Located off the west coast of mainland Scotland, the Isle of Skye is the largest and northernmost of the Inner Hebrides. The island is connected to the mainland by the Skye Bridge, making it easily accessible for visitors. Despite its accessibility, Skye retains an air of remoteness and mystery, with its ever-changing weather and dramatic landscapes contributing to its ethereal beauty.

The island is approximately 50 miles long and 25 miles wide, offering a diverse range of scenery, from the jagged peaks of the Cuillin mountains to the rolling moorlands and pristine beaches. Skye's name is derived from the Old Norse word "sky-a," meaning "cloud island," which perfectly encapsulates the island's mist-shrouded hills and moody atmosphere.

Portree: The Heart of the Isle of Skye

Portree, the island's capital and largest town, is the perfect starting point for exploring Skye. Nestled around a picturesque harbour, Portree is a charming town with pastel-coloured houses, cosy pubs, and a vibrant arts scene. Despite its small size, Portree offers all the amenities a traveller might need, including accommodations, restaurants, shops, and tour operators.

Things to Do in Portree:

The Harbour: The bustling harbour is the focal point of Portree, where fishing boats bob in the water, and tourists and locals alike gather to enjoy the views. From here, you can take boat trips to explore the surrounding coastline, offering opportunities for wildlife spotting, including seals, dolphins, and seabirds.

The Lump: A short walk from the harbour takes you to The Lump, a wooded promontory that offers panoramic views over Portree and the surrounding hills. The viewpoint is particularly stunning at sunset when the sky and sea are bathed in golden light.

Aros Centre: For those interested in Skye's culture and history, the Aros Centre on the outskirts of Portree is a must-visit. The centre hosts exhibitions, film screenings, and live performances, with a focus on Gaelic culture and the island's natural environment.

The Old Man of Storr: Skye's Most Famous Landmark

No visit to the Isle of Skye is complete without seeing the Old Man of Storr, one of the island's most iconic and photographed landmarks. The Old Man of Storr is a towering pinnacle of rock that rises dramatically from the Trotternish Ridge, a geological feature that stretches along the northeastern coast of Skye.

Hiking to the Old Man of Storr:

The hike to the Old Man of Storr is one of the most popular walks on the island, offering stunning views and a sense of awe as you approach the towering rock formations. The trail is approximately 3.8 kilometres (2.4 miles) round trip and is moderately challenging, with a steep ascent that rewards you with breathtaking vistas over the Sound of Raasay and the surrounding landscape.

The Landscape: The area around the Old Man of Storr is characterized by its otherworldly landscape, with jagged rock formations, sweeping moorlands, and distant mountains creating a scene that feels almost surreal. The Old Man of Storr itself is surrounded by smaller pinnacles and cliffs, adding to the dramatic atmosphere.

Photography: The Old Man of Storr is a photographer's dream, especially in the early morning or late afternoon when the light is soft and the shadows accentuate the rugged terrain. The site is often shrouded in mist, adding to its mystique, but when the skies clear, the views are truly unforgettable.

The Quiraing: A Geological Wonder

The Quiraing is another of Skye's remarkable geological features, located on the northernmost peninsula of the island, known as the Trotternish Ridge. The Quiraing is a landslip, a massive area of unstable land that has created an extraordinary landscape of cliffs, plateaus, and pinnacles. It is one of the most dramatic and visually stunning areas on the Isle of Skye, offering incredible hiking opportunities and breathtaking views.

Exploring the Quiraing:

The Quiraing can be explored on foot via a circular hike that is approximately 6.8 kilometres (4.2 miles) long. The trail is relatively challenging, with steep sections and uneven terrain, but the effort is well worth it for the spectacular scenery.

The Path: The path around the Quiraing takes you through a series of natural features with evocative names like the Needle, the Prison, and the Table. Each of these features adds to the sense of being in a place unlike any other, with the landscape constantly changing as you move along the trail.

The Views: From the highest points on the trail, you are treated to panoramic views over the island's northern coastline, the surrounding sea, and the distant mountains of mainland Scotland. The Quiraing is a place where the power of nature is on full display, with the landscape shaped by millennia of geological forces.

Photography and Wildlife: Like the Old Man of Storr, the Quiraing is a favourite spot for photographers, with its unique formations providing endless opportunities for capturing the beauty of Skye. The area is also rich in wildlife, with golden eagles, red deer, and a variety of seabirds often spotted in the vicinity.

The Fairy Pools: A Magical Highland Retreat

The Fairy Pools are a series of crystal-clear, blue-green pools and waterfalls located at the foot of the Black Cuillin mountains, near the village of Carbost. These enchanting pools have become one of Skye's most popular attractions, drawing visitors with their ethereal beauty and the promise of a refreshing dip in the pristine waters.

Visiting the Fairy Pools:

The Fairy Pools are easily accessible via a short hike from the car park at Glen Brittle. The walk to the pools is approximately 2.4 kilometres (1.5 miles) round trip, making it suitable for most fitness levels. The path follows the course of the River Brittle, with several opportunities to cross the river via stepping stones.

The Pools: The Fairy Pools are known for their vibrant colours, which range from deep blues to emerald greens, depending on the light and the angle of the sun. The pools are fed by a series of waterfalls that cascade down from the Cuillin mountains, creating a picturesque scene that feels almost otherworldly.

Swimming: For the brave and hardy, the Fairy Pools offer the chance to take a dip in some of the clearest and coldest water in Scotland. While the water is chilly, especially outside of the summer months, the experience of swimming in such a magical setting is truly unforgettable.

Photography: The Fairy Pools are a photographer's paradise, with the clear waters and surrounding mountains providing a perfect backdrop for stunning landscape shots. Early morning or late afternoon light often enhances the colours of the pools, making for particularly striking images.

Dunvegan Castle: A Historic Highland Stronghold

Dunvegan Castle, the oldest continuously inhabited castle in Scotland, is a must-visit for anyone interested in the island's history and heritage. Located on the west coast of Skye, near the village of Dunvegan, the castle has been the ancestral home of the Chiefs of Clan MacLeod for over 800 years.

Exploring Dunvegan Castle:

Dunvegan Castle is a fascinating blend of history, architecture, and natural beauty. The castle's impressive façade and its stunning location on the shores of Loch Dunvegan make it one of the most iconic landmarks on the Isle of Skye.

The Castle Interior: Visitors can explore the castle's interior, which is filled with historical artifacts, paintings, and memorabilia related to Clan MacLeod. Highlights include the Fairy Flag, a precious relic believed to have magical properties, and the Dunvegan Cup, an ancient ceremonial drinking vessel.

The Gardens: The castle is surrounded by beautifully landscaped gardens, which offer a peaceful retreat and a contrast to the wild landscapes that characterize much of the island. The gardens feature a variety of plant species, water features, and walking paths, making them a delightful place to explore.

Boat Trips: From the castle, you can take a boat trip to Loch Dunvegan to see the seal colony that lives in the waters around the castle. The loch is home to a large number of seals, and the boat trips provide a unique opportunity to observe these playful creatures in their natural habitat.

Talisker Distillery: A Taste of Skye

No visit to the Isle of Skye would be complete without sampling some of its famous whisky, and Talisker Distillery is the perfect place to do so. Located in the village of Carbost, Talisker is the oldest distillery on the island and is renowned for its rich, peaty single malts that capture the essence of Skye.

Visiting Talisker Distillery:

Distillery Tours: Talisker offers guided tours that take you through the whisky-making process, from the mashing and fermentation to the distillation and maturation. The tour concludes with a tasting session, where you can sample some of Talisker's finest whiskies.

The Whisky: Talisker's whiskies are known for their distinctive smoky flavour, with notes of sea salt, pepper, and peat that evoke the rugged landscapes and coastal environment of Skye. A visit to the distillery provides a deeper appreciation for the craftsmanship and tradition that goes into each bottle.

The Surroundings: The distillery is located in a picturesque setting, with views over Loch Harport and the Cuillin mountains in the distance. After your tour, take some time to explore the surrounding area, or relax with a dram of whisky while taking in the stunning scenery.

The Scottish Borders

The Scottish Borders, often overlooked in favour of Scotland's more famous highland and island regions, is a land rich in history, culture, and natural beauty. This historic region, located just south of Edinburgh and stretching to the English border, is known for its rolling hills, picturesque villages, and a legacy that includes some of Scotland's most significant abbeys and textile heritage. The Scottish Borders is a place where history and legend intertwine, where every hill and river seems to whisper tales of battles, monks, and weavers. In this chapter, we will explore the charms of the Scottish Borders, uncovering its abbeys, landscapes, and the enduring influence of its textile industry.

Introduction to the Scottish Borders

The Scottish Borders is a region that has played a crucial role in Scotland's history, particularly during the turbulent times of the Wars of Scottish Independence and the Border Reivers. It is a land where the past feels very present, with ruins of ancient abbeys, castles, and battlefields dotting the landscape. The region is characterized by its gently rolling hills, lush valleys, and winding rivers, creating a pastoral scene that has inspired poets and artists for centuries.

The Borders are also known for their rich textile heritage, particularly in woollen goods, thanks to the region's long history of sheep farming. The textile towns of the Borders, such as Galashiels, Hawick, and Selkirk, have been central to Scotland's woollen industry, producing high-quality tweed, cashmere, and other fabrics that are celebrated worldwide.

Historic Abbeys: A Glimpse into Medieval Scotland

The Scottish Borders is home to some of Scotland's most significant and beautifully preserved abbeys, each with its own unique history and architectural style. These abbeys are not only religious sites but also monuments to the region's turbulent past, particularly during the Border Wars between Scotland and England.

Melrose Abbey:

Perhaps the most famous of the Border Abbeys, Melrose Abbey is a stunning example of Gothic architecture and a must-visit for anyone interested in Scotland's medieval history. Founded in 1136 by King David I, the abbey was home to Cistercian monks and quickly became one of the wealthiest and most powerful abbeys in Scotland. Despite being repeatedly attacked and partially destroyed during the Border Wars, much of the abbey's intricate stonework remains intact, offering a glimpse into its former glory.

The Heart of Robert the Bruce: One of the most intriguing aspects of Melrose Abbey is its connection to Robert the Bruce, one of Scotland's greatest heroes. It is believed that the embalmed heart of Robert the Bruce was buried at Melrose Abbey, a fact commemorated by a modern stone marker within the abbey grounds.

Exploring the Abbey: Visitors to Melrose Abbey can wander through the ruins, admiring the ornate stone carvings of saints, dragons, and other creatures that adorn the walls. The abbey's grounds are also home to a small museum that houses artefacts discovered during archaeological excavations.

Jedburgh Abbey:

Jedburgh Abbey is another of the great Border abbeys, known for its impressive scale and beautifully preserved nave. Founded in the 12th century, Jedburgh Abbey was originally a priory before being elevated to the status of an abbey. Like Melrose, Jedburgh suffered during the Border Wars but retains much of its original grandeur.

The Nave and Choir: The abbey's nave is particularly striking, with its soaring arches and intricate stonework. The choir, with its large east window, offers a serene space for reflection and provides insight into the abbey's religious significance.

Visitor Experience: The visitor centre at Jedburgh Abbey offers an excellent introduction to the history of the abbey and the role it plays in the local community. The centre also features a collection of artefacts, including medieval stone carvings and relics from the abbey's past.

Dryburgh Abbey:

Nestled in a peaceful loop of the River Tweed, Dryburgh Abbey is perhaps the most picturesque of the Border abbeys. Surrounded by woodlands and gardens, Dryburgh offers a tranquil escape and a chance to explore one of Scotland's most romantic ruins. Founded in the 12th century, the abbey was home to Premonstratensian canons and, like its neighbours, suffered during the Border Wars.

Sir Walter Scott's Resting Place: Dryburgh Abbey is the final resting place of Sir Walter Scott, the famous Scottish novelist and poet. Scott had a deep connection to the Borders, and his burial at Dryburgh is a fitting tribute to his love for the region.

Exploring Dryburgh: The abbey's setting makes it a perfect spot for a stroll, with the ruins blending harmoniously with the surrounding landscape. The chapter house, with its intact stone vaulting, is particularly well-preserved and offers a glimpse into the abbey's architectural splendour.

Kelso Abbey:

Although not as well-preserved as the other Border abbeys, Kelso Abbey's ruins are still impressive, hinting at its former grandeur. Founded in the 12th century, Kelso Abbey was one of the largest and richest abbeys in Scotland. Its strategic location near the English border made it a frequent target during the Border Wars, leading to its eventual decline.

Romanesque Architecture: Kelso Abbey is notable for its Romanesque architecture, particularly its west front, which features a large, arched doorway flanked by decorative stonework. The abbey's design influenced many other ecclesiastical buildings in Scotland and beyond.

Exploring Kelso: Visitors to Kelso Abbey can explore the remaining ruins, including parts of the nave and the chapter house. The abbey's location in the heart of Kelso makes it an easy stop while exploring the town's other attractions, such as Floors Castle and the Roxburghe Estate.

The Rolling Hills and Scenic Landscapes

The natural beauty of the Scottish Borders is one of its greatest attractions, with the region's rolling hills, lush valleys, and meandering rivers providing a stunning backdrop for outdoor activities. The landscape is ideal for walking, cycling, and wildlife watching, with a network of trails and paths that take you through some of Scotland's most idyllic countryside.

The Cheviot Hills:

The Cheviot Hills, which straddle the border between Scotland and England, are a prominent feature of the Borders' landscape. These rolling hills offer a mix of gentle slopes and more challenging peaks, making them popular with walkers and hikers.

Walking Trails: The Southern Upland Way, a long-distance walking trail, passes through the Cheviots, offering stunning views and the chance to explore the region's rich flora and fauna. The St. Cuthbert's Way, another popular trail, links Melrose to Lindisfarne in Northumberland, crossing the Cheviots along the way.

Wildlife Watching: The Cheviots are home to a variety of wildlife, including red deer, otters, and a wide range of bird species. Birdwatchers will particularly enjoy spotting the skylarks, curlews, and peregrine falcons that frequent the area.

The River Tweed:

The River Tweed is one of Scotland's most famous rivers, known for its salmon fishing and scenic beauty. Flowing through the heart of the Borders, the Tweed is lined with charming villages, historic sites, and picturesque countryside.

Fishing on the Tweed: The River Tweed is renowned for its salmon fishing, attracting anglers from around the world. The fishing season typically runs from February to November, with several beats (stretches of river) available for both experienced and novice anglers.

Exploring the Riverbanks: The banks of the Tweed are dotted with walking trails and cycling paths, offering the perfect way to explore the river and its surroundings. The Tweed Valley Forest Park, located near Peebles, is a great place for outdoor activities, with trails ranging from easy strolls to more challenging hikes.

The Eildon Hills:

The Eildon Hills, located near Melrose, are one of the most iconic features of the Borders' landscape. These three distinctive peaks are a popular destination for walkers, offering panoramic views over the surrounding countryside.

Walking the Eildons: The Eildon Hills can be explored via a network of trails that cater to different fitness levels. The most popular route takes you to the summit of Eildon Hill North, the highest of the three peaks, where you can enjoy breathtaking views that stretch as far as the Cheviots and the North Sea.

Historical Significance: The Eildon Hills are steeped in history, with evidence of ancient settlements and Roman camps found on their slopes.

The hills are also associated with Arthurian legend, adding an element of myth and mystery to your hike.

Textile Heritage: Weaving the Fabric of the Borders

The Scottish Borders has a long and proud tradition of textile production, particularly in woollen goods. The region's abundant supply of sheep, combined with a skilled workforce, made the Borders a hub of the Scottish woollen industry. Today, the towns of the Borders continue to produce high-quality textiles, with several mills and factories still in operation.

Hawick: The Cashmere Capital

Hawick, one of the largest towns in the Borders, is renowned for its production of cashmere and knitwear. The town has a rich industrial heritage, with many of its mills dating back to the 18th and 19th centuries.

Mill Tours: Several of Hawick's mills offer guided tours, providing visitors with an insight into the textile production process. Tours typically include a visit to the factory floor, where you can see the machines in action, as well as a chance to purchase high-quality cashmere products directly from the source.

The Borders Textile Towerhouse: Located in the heart of Hawick, the Borders Textile Towerhouse is a museum dedicated to the region's textile heritage. The museum features exhibits on the history of textile production in the Borders, as well as displays of vintage knitwear and contemporary fashion.

Galashiels: The Heart of the Tweed Industry

Galashiels is another important textile town in the Borders, known for its production of tweed. The town's mills have been producing this iconic Scottish fabric for centuries, and Galashiels continues to be a centre of the industry today.

The Great Tapestry of Scotland: Galashiels is home to the Great Tapestry of Scotland, one of the largest community arts projects in the world. The tapestry, which tells the story of Scotland's history from prehistoric times to the present day, is displayed in a purpose-built gallery in the town.

Tweed Tours: Several of Galashiels' tweed mills offer tours, allowing visitors to learn about the intricate process of weaving tweed. You'll have the opportunity to see the looms in action and discover how the unique patterns and colours of tweed are created.

CHAPTER 4

SCOTLAND'S HIDDEN GEMS

Less-Known Islands

Scotland is renowned for its majestic landscapes, historic cities, and iconic sites, but beyond the well-trodden paths lie hidden treasures waiting to be discovered. Among these are Scotland's lesser-known islands, a collection of remote, rugged, and breathtakingly beautiful lands that offer a unique glimpse into the country's natural beauty, history, and culture. While the Isle of Skye and the Inner Hebrides might draw the most attention, islands like Orkney, Shetland, and the lesser-visited parts of the Hebrides hold an unmatched charm. These islands are the perfect destinations for those seeking tranquillity, adventure, and a deeper connection with Scotland's wild heart.

The Orkney Islands: A Journey Through Time and Nature

Located off the northeastern coast of Scotland, the Orkney Islands are an archipelago rich in history, archaeology, and natural beauty. The islands have been inhabited for over 8,500 years, and evidence of their ancient past is found in the numerous Neolithic sites that dot the landscape. Orkney is also a place of rugged cliffs, sweeping beaches, and vibrant wildlife, making it a paradise for nature lovers and history enthusiasts alike.

Skara Brae: Neolithic Wonders

One of Orkney's most famous attractions is Skara Brae, a remarkably well-preserved Neolithic village that dates back over 5,000 years. Often referred to as the "Scottish Pompeii," Skara Brae offers an unparalleled glimpse into the lives of prehistoric people. The village, buried in sand until its discovery in the 19th century, features stone houses complete with furniture, hearths, and storage areas.

Visitor Experience: A visit to Skara Brae begins at the visitor centre, where you can learn about the history of the site and view a replica of one of the houses. From there, a short walk takes you to the actual ruins, where you can explore the ancient dwellings and imagine life in Neolithic times.

The Ring of Brodgar: A Mystical Stone Circle

The Ring of Brodgar is another of Orkney's ancient marvels. This large stone circle, believed to date from between 2500 and 2000 BC, is part of the Heart of Neolithic Orkney UNESCO World Heritage Site. The ring is composed of 27 standing stones (though it originally had 60), arranged in a perfect circle with a diameter of 104 meters (341 feet). The exact purpose of the Ring of Brodgar remains a mystery, but it is thought to have been used for religious or ceremonial purposes.

Exploring the Ring: The site is open to visitors year-round, and walking among the towering stones is a powerful experience. The surrounding landscape, with its lochs and hills, adds to the sense of mysticism and awe that the ring evokes.

The Italian Chapel: A Story of Resilience and Faith

One of the more unexpected sites on Orkney is the Italian Chapel, a small but beautifully ornate church built by Italian prisoners of war during World War II. The chapel was constructed from two Nissen huts, with the interior meticulously decorated with painted frescoes and wrought ironwork. The chapel stands as a testament to the resilience, faith, and artistry of the prisoners who built it, and it has become a symbol of peace and reconciliation.

Visiting the Chapel: The Italian Chapel is located on Lamb Holm, one of the smaller islands connected to the Orkney mainland by the Churchill Barriers. The chapel is open to visitors, and its interior, with its intricate artwork, is a moving and inspirational sight.

Orkney's Natural Wonders: Cliff Walks and Wildlife Watching

Beyond its historical sites, Orkney is also known for its stunning natural beauty. The islands are home to dramatic cliffs, sandy beaches, and a rich array of wildlife. The towering cliffs of Yesnaby, for example, offer breathtaking views over the Atlantic Ocean and are a popular spot for birdwatching, particularly during the summer when seabirds like puffins, guillemots, and kittiwakes nest on the cliffs.

The Old Man of Hoy: One of Orkney's most iconic natural landmarks is the Old Man of Hoy, a towering sea stack that rises nearly 137 meters (449 feet) from the ocean. The Old Man is a popular challenge for experienced climbers, but for most visitors, the best way to experience it is by taking the scenic walk from Rackwick Bay, which offers stunning views of the stack and the surrounding coastline.

Wildlife Watching: Orkney is a haven for wildlife enthusiasts, with opportunities to see seals, otters, and various bird species. The islands are also one of the best places in Scotland to spot orcas, which can sometimes be seen off the coast, especially in the summer months.

The Shetland Islands: Scotland's Northern Frontier

Farther north than Orkney, the Shetland Islands are Scotland's northernmost point, closer to Norway than to Edinburgh. The Shetlands are a land of rugged beauty, Viking heritage, and a unique culture that blends Scottish and Scandinavian influences. With their dramatic cliffs, windswept moors, and pristine beaches, the Shetlands offer a truly remote and wild experience.

Lerwick: The Heart of Shetland

Lerwick, the capital of Shetland, is a bustling town with a rich history and a vibrant cultural scene. The town's harbour, with its colourful boats and historic buildings, is the perfect starting point for exploring the islands.

Shetland Museum and Archives: To get a sense of Shetland's history and culture, a visit to the Shetland Museum and Archives is a must. The museum's exhibits cover everything from the islands' geology and natural history to their Viking past and fishing heritage. The museum also houses a collection of traditional Shetland textiles, including the famous Shetland lace.

Up Helly Aa: One of Shetland's most famous events is the Up Helly Aa fire festival, held annually in Lerwick to celebrate the island's Viking heritage. The festival culminates in a torch-lit procession and the burning of a Viking longship, followed by a night of celebrations. It's a unique and unforgettable experience for visitors lucky enough to be in Shetland during the festival.

Jarlshof: A Journey Through Shetland's Past

One of the most important archaeological sites in Shetland is Jarlshof, located on the southern tip of the mainland. Jarlshof is an extraordinary site that spans over 4,000 years of history, with remains from the Neolithic, Bronze Age, Iron Age, Norse, and Medieval periods all found in one location.

Exploring Jarlshof: Visitors to Jarlshof can walk among the ruins of ancient houses, brochs (Iron Age towers), Viking longhouses, and a medieval farmstead. The site is incredibly well-preserved, and interpretive signs help bring the history of Jarlshof to life.

Shetland's Natural Wonders: Coastal Cliffs and Seabird Colonies

Shetland is known for its dramatic coastal scenery, with towering cliffs, sea stacks, and sheltered bays providing a stunning backdrop for outdoor activities. The islands are also home to some of the largest seabird colonies in the UK, making them a paradise for birdwatchers.

Hermaness Nature Reserve: Located on the northernmost tip of Shetland's mainland, Hermaness Nature Reserve is one of the best places to experience the islands' wild beauty. The reserve is home to vast seabird colonies, including gannets, puffins, and skuas. The cliffs at Hermaness are also a great place to spot marine mammals, including seals and occasionally orcas.

The Noup of Noss: Another spectacular birdwatching site is the Noup of Noss, a sheer cliff on the island of Noss. The cliffs are home to thousands of nesting seabirds, including guillemots, razorbills, and fulmars. Boat trips around the island offer close-up views of the cliffs and their avian inhabitants.

The Outer Hebrides: A World of Unspoiled Beauty

The Outer Hebrides, also known as the Western Isles, are a chain of islands located off the west coast of mainland Scotland. The islands are known for their unspoiled landscapes, including white sandy beaches, rugged mountains, and vast moorlands. The Outer Hebrides are also steeped in Gaelic culture, with the Gaelic language still spoken by many of the islands' inhabitants.

Lewis and Harris: A Tale of Two Islands

The Isle of Lewis and Harris, though often referred to as separate islands, are part of the same landmass. Lewis, the northern part, is known for its rich history and cultural heritage, while Harris, to the south, is famous for its stunning beaches and dramatic landscapes.

Callanish Standing Stones: One of the most iconic sites on Lewis is the Callanish Standing Stones, a prehistoric stone circle that dates back over 5,000 years. The stones are arranged in a cruciform pattern, with a central circle surrounded by rows of standing stones. The purpose of the stones remains a mystery, but they are believed to have been used for ritual or ceremonial purposes.

Luskentyre Beach: On Harris, Luskentyre Beach is often hailed as one of the most beautiful beaches in the world. With its white sands and turquoise waters, Luskentyre could easily be mistaken for a tropical paradise, yet it retains a wild and rugged charm that is distinctly Scottish.

The Uists and Benbecula: Islands of Tranquility

The islands of North Uist, South Uist, and Benbecula are known for their tranquil landscapes and rich wildlife. The islands are dotted with lochs, peat bogs, and machair (fertile grasslands), making them ideal for walking, birdwatching, and enjoying the peace and solitude of the Hebrides.

Balranald Nature Reserve: Located on North Uist, Balranald Nature Reserve is one of the best places in the Outer Hebrides to see wildlife. The reserve is home to a variety of bird species, including corncrakes, lapwings, and redshanks. The machair flowers in the summer create a colourful tapestry of wildflowers, attracting both birds and visitors alike.

Loch Druidibeg Nature Reserve: On South Uist, Loch Druidibeg Nature Reserve is a haven for wildlife, particularly birds of prey like golden eagles and hen harriers. The reserve's diverse habitats, including moorland, peat bog, and lochs, support a wide range of flora and fauna.

Barra: The Jewel of the Southern Isles

Barra, the southernmost inhabited island of the Outer Hebrides, is often described as one of the most picturesque islands in Scotland. With its rolling hills, sandy beaches, and clear waters, Barra is a paradise for outdoor enthusiasts and those seeking a peaceful retreat.

Kisimul Castle: One of Barra's most iconic landmarks is Kisimul Castle, a medieval fortress that stands on a rocky islet in the middle of Castlebay. The castle is accessible by boat and offers a fascinating glimpse into Barra's history and the Clan MacNeil, who ruled the island for centuries.

Traigh Mhor Beach: Barra is also home to one of the world's most unusual airports, located on Traigh Mhor Beach. The airport's runway is the beach itself, and flights are scheduled around the tides. Watching a plane take off or land on the beach is a unique experience that can only be found in Barra.

Historic Villages and Towns

Scotland's landscapes are not only adorned with dramatic mountains and serene lochs but also dotted with picturesque villages and towns steeped in history. While cities like Edinburgh and Glasgow often steal the spotlight, countless smaller destinations offer a glimpse into Scotland's rich past and unique culture. In this section, we'll take a closer look at some of Scotland's most charming historic villages and lesser-known towns, including Pitlochry, St Andrews, and Dunkeld, each offering a unique blend of natural beauty, architectural heritage, and cultural significance.

Pitlochry: The Gateway to the Highlands

Nestled at the heart of Scotland, Pitlochry is a quintessential Highland town known for its Victorian charm, scenic surroundings, and warm hospitality. Situated on the banks of the River Tummel and surrounded by rolling hills, Pitlochry has been a popular destination since Queen

Victoria's visit in the mid-19th century. Today, it continues to attract visitors with its mix of outdoor activities, historical attractions, and vibrant cultural scene.

The Pitlochry Festival Theatre: A Cultural Hub

One of Pitlochry's most significant cultural landmarks is the Pitlochry Festival Theatre, often referred to as the "Theatre in the Hills." Established in 1951, this renowned theatre offers a diverse program of performances, from classic plays to contemporary works, drawing audiences from across the country. The theatre's stunning location, set against the backdrop of the Highlands, adds to the experience, making it a must-visit for culture lovers.

Visitor Experience: The theatre's season typically runs from May to October, with performances held in an intimate auditorium. In addition to the main productions, the theatre also hosts concerts, talks, and workshops, providing a rich cultural offering throughout the year.

Blair Castle: A Journey Through Time

Just a short drive from Pitlochry, Blair Castle is one of Scotland's most impressive and historically significant castles. The ancestral home of the Dukes of Atholl, Blair Castle has a history spanning over 700 years and has played a key role in many of Scotland's historical events. The castle's interior is filled with an extraordinary collection of arms, armour, and fine furnishings, while its extensive gardens and grounds offer a peaceful retreat.

Exploring Blair Castle: Visitors can explore the castle's grand rooms, including the opulent Ballroom and the medieval Great Hall, and learn about the Atholl family's fascinating history. The castle grounds also include the Hercules Garden, a beautifully restored walled garden, and the Diana's Grove, home to some of the tallest trees in Britain.

Outdoor Adventures: From Hillwalking to Water Sports

Pitlochry's location makes it an ideal base for exploring the surrounding natural beauty of the Highlands. The area offers a wide range of outdoor activities, from hillwalking and cycling to fishing and water sports.

Ben Vrackie: One of the most popular walks in the area is the ascent of Ben Vrackie, an 841-meter (2,759-foot) peak that offers stunning views over Pitlochry and the surrounding countryside. The walk is challenging but rewarding, with a well-marked path leading to the summit.

Loch Faskally: For a more leisurely experience, visitors can take a stroll around Loch Faskally, a man-made reservoir created by the construction of the Pitlochry Dam. The loch is popular for fishing and boating, and the surrounding woodlands are home to a variety of wildlife, making it a great spot for nature walks.

St Andrews: The Home of Golf and Ancient Learning

St Andrews is a name synonymous with golf, history, and education. Located on the east coast of Fife, this ancient town is home to the University of St Andrews, the oldest university in Scotland, and the famous St Andrews Links, often referred to as the "Home of Golf." But beyond its academic and sporting reputation, St Andrews is a charming town with a rich history, stunning coastal scenery, and a lively cultural scene.

St Andrews Cathedral: A Window into Medieval Scotland

The ruins of St Andrews Cathedral, once the largest and most magnificent church in Scotland, stand as a testament to the town's medieval past. The cathedral was founded in 1158 and served as the centre of the Catholic Church in Scotland for centuries. Today, the ruins offer a glimpse into the grandeur of the cathedral's former glory, with its towering walls and ornate stonework.

Visitor Experience: Visitors can explore the ruins and climb St Rule's Tower, which offers panoramic views over St Andrews and the surrounding countryside. The adjacent museum houses a collection of medieval artefacts, including intricately carved stones and religious relics.

The Old Course: Walking in the Footsteps of Legends

For golf enthusiasts, no visit to St Andrews is complete without a pilgrimage to the Old Course, the oldest and most famous golf course in the world. The Old Course has been the site of numerous historic moments in golf, and its iconic features, such as the Swilcan Bridge and the Road Hole, are known to golfers around the globe.

Playing the Old Course: While playing the Old Course is a dream for many, it's also possible to take a guided tour of the course or simply walk the paths that legends of the game have trodden. The nearby British Golf Museum provides further insight into the history of the sport and its deep connection to St Andrews.

West Sands Beach: Coastal Beauty and Outdoor Fun

West Sands Beach, located just a short walk from the town centre, is one of Scotland's most beautiful beaches. With its wide expanse of golden sand and views over the North Sea, West Sands is a popular spot for walking, picnicking, and even swimming for those brave enough to face the chilly waters.

Film Connection: The beach is also famous for its appearance in the opening scenes of the Oscar-winning film Chariots of Fire. Visitors can take a stroll along the sands or simply enjoy the views of the sea and the historic town.

Dunkeld: A Charming Riverside Town with a Rich Heritage

Situated on the banks of the River Tay in Perthshire, Dunkeld is one of Scotland's most picturesque and historically significant villages. With its charming whitewashed houses, ancient cathedral, and beautiful riverside setting, Dunkeld offers a perfect blend of natural beauty and historical intrigue. The village is often described as the gateway to the Highlands and serves as an ideal base for exploring the surrounding countryside.

Dunkeld Cathedral: A Spiritual and Historical Landmark

The most prominent feature of Dunkeld is its cathedral, which dates back to the 12th century. Dunkeld Cathedral is a unique blend of Gothic and Norman architecture, with part of the building still used as a parish church. The cathedral's setting, nestled among ancient trees on the banks of the River Tay, adds to its serene and spiritual atmosphere.

Exploring the Cathedral: Visitors can explore the cathedral's ruins, including the choir and nave, as well as the more intact sections that house an impressive collection of medieval relics. The cathedral's grounds are a peaceful place for reflection, with stunning views over the river.

The Hermitage: A Woodland Walk to Remember

Just a short distance from Dunkeld lies The Hermitage, a beautiful woodland area that offers some of the most scenic walks in Scotland. The Hermitage is home to towering Douglas firs, some of the tallest trees in Britain, as well as picturesque waterfalls and historic follies.

Ossian's Hall: One of the highlights of The Hermitage is Ossian's Hall, an 18th-century folly built to honour the legendary Scottish poet Ossian. The hall overlooks the dramatic Black Linn Falls on the River Braan, and its mirrored interior creates a stunning visual effect, reflecting the surrounding natural beauty.

Dunkel's Historic Buildings and Artisan Shops

Dunkeld's town centre is a delight to explore, with its well-preserved historic buildings and independent shops. The village's architecture reflects its long history, with many of the buildings dating back to the 18th century.

The Little Houses Improvement Scheme: Much of Dunkeld's charm is due to the Little Houses Improvement Scheme, a restoration project undertaken in the 1950s to preserve the village's historic buildings. The scheme was a success, and today, Dunkeld's streets are lined with beautifully restored cottages and townhouses, many of which are now home to artisan shops, galleries, and cafes.

Local Crafts: Dunkeld is known for its thriving arts and crafts scene, and visitors will find a range of locally made products, from pottery and jewellery to textiles and artwork. The village's shops and galleries offer a chance to take home a piece of Scotland's rich artistic heritage.

Natural Wonders

Scotland is renowned for its rugged landscapes, dramatic coastlines, and breathtaking natural beauty. While iconic locations like Loch Ness, Ben

Nevis, and the Isle of Skye attract thousands of visitors each year, there are many lesser-known natural wonders scattered across the country that are equally captivating. In this section, we'll explore some of Scotland's hidden gems, from the mystical Fairy Pools and the enchanting Fingal's Cave to the vast wilderness of Cairngorms National Park. These destinations offer a deeper connection to Scotland's untamed landscapes and a chance to experience nature in its purest form.

Fairy Pools: The Enchanting Waters of Skye

Tucked away in the rugged Cuillin Mountains on the Isle of Skye, the Fairy Pools are a series of crystal-clear, turquoise-coloured pools and waterfalls that have become a must-see for nature lovers and photographers alike. These magical pools are fed by the waters of the River Brittle and are surrounded by some of the most stunning mountain scenery in Scotland.

The Allure of the Fairy Pools

The Fairy Pools are named for their ethereal beauty, which is said to be so enchanting that it could only have been created by fairies. The vibrant hues of the water, which range from deep blue to emerald green, are set against a backdrop of dark volcanic rock, creating a striking contrast that is truly mesmerizing. On sunny days, the water sparkles and shimmers, making the pools appear almost otherworldly.

Hiking to the Pools: Reaching the Fairy Pools requires a moderate hike through Glen Brittle, a journey that takes about 20-30 minutes from the car park. The trail winds through heather-covered moorland and crosses small streams before arriving at the first of the pools. As you continue along the path, you'll encounter more pools and cascading waterfalls, each more beautiful than the last.

Swimming in the Fairy Pools: While the water may look inviting, it is also incredibly cold, even in the summer. However, for those who are brave enough, taking a dip in the Fairy Pools is an invigorating experience. The clarity of the water allows you to see every detail of the rocks beneath the surface, adding to the sense of wonder.

Photography and Wildlife: The Fairy Pools are a photographer's dream, offering countless opportunities to capture the stunning landscapes and the vibrant colours of the water. Wildlife enthusiasts may also spot red deer, rabbits, and a variety of bird species in the surrounding area.

The Legend of the Fairy Pools

Local folklore adds to the mystique of the Fairy Pools. According to legend, the pools were created by the faeries who once lived in the Cuillin Mountains. These magical beings were said to have bathed in the pools and used their waters for healing. Even today, the Fairy Pools are believed to possess a certain magical quality that draws visitors from around the world.

Fingal's Cave: A Natural Cathedral of the Sea

Located on the uninhabited island of Staffa, off the west coast of Scotland, Fingal's Cave is one of the most remarkable geological formations in the world. This sea cave, formed from hexagonal basalt columns, is famous for its cathedral-like interior and its unique acoustics, which have inspired artists, musicians, and poets for centuries.

The Geological Wonder of Fingal's Cave

Fingal's Cave was formed millions of years ago during a period of intense volcanic activity. As the lava from ancient eruptions cooled and contracted, it created the distinctive hexagonal columns that make up the walls of the cave. These columns are similar to those found at the Giant's Causeway in Northern Ireland, as the same geological processes formed both sites.

Exploring the Cave: Visitors can explore Fingal's Cave by taking a boat tour from the nearby Isle of Mull or Oban. The boat ride offers stunning views of the Scottish coastline and the chance to spot marine wildlife such as dolphins, seals, and puffins. Once on the island, a short walk leads to the cave's entrance, where you can venture inside and experience its awe-inspiring beauty.

The Sound of Fingal's Cave: One of the most unique aspects of Fingal's Cave is its acoustics. The shape and structure of the cave create a natural echo chamber, amplifying the sound of the waves crashing against the walls. This eerie and haunting sound has inspired many, including composer Felix Mendelssohn, who wrote the Hebrides Overture after visiting the cave in 1829.

The Legend of Fingal's Cave

Fingal's Cave is named after the legendary Celtic hero Fionn mac Cumhaill (Finn McCool), who is said to have created the cave as part of a bridge between Scotland and Ireland. According to the myth, Fionn was a giant who built the bridge so that he could fight another giant in Ireland. The legend adds a layer of mystery and intrigue to the cave, making it a must-visit for those interested in both natural beauty and folklore.

Cairngorms National Park: Scotland's Wild Heart

Cairngorms National Park, located in the heart of the Scottish Highlands, is the largest national park in the United Kingdom and one of Scotland's most spectacular natural landscapes. Covering an area of over 4,500 square kilometres, the park is a vast wilderness of mountains, forests, rivers, and lochs, offering endless opportunities for outdoor adventure and exploration.

The Majestic Mountains of the Cairngorms

The park is named after the Cairngorm Mountains, a range of ancient, weathered peaks that dominate the landscape. The highest of these is Ben Macdui, which stands at 1,309 meters (4,295 feet) and is the second-highest mountain in the UK. The Cairngorms are a haven for hikers, climbers, and nature lovers, with trails that range from gentle woodland walks to challenging mountain ascents.

Hiking and Climbing: The Cairngorms offer some of the best hiking and climbing in Scotland, with routes that cater to all levels of experience. For those seeking a challenge, the ascent of Ben Macdui is a rewarding experience, offering panoramic views of the surrounding mountains and valleys. The park is also home to several other Munros (mountains over 3,000 feet), including Braeriach and Cairn Gorm.

Wildlife Watching: Cairngorms National Park is one of the best places in Scotland to see native wildlife. The park is home to a variety of species, including red deer, golden eagles, ospreys, and the elusive Scottish wildcat. The ancient Caledonian pine forests within the park are particularly rich in biodiversity, offering a habitat for species such as red squirrels and capercaillie.

The Lochs and Rivers of the Cairngorms

In addition to its mountains, the Cairngorms are also known for their pristine lochs and rivers. These bodies of water add to the park's beauty and provide opportunities for activities such as fishing, kayaking, and wild swimming.

Loch Morlich: Loch Morlich, located near the town of Aviemore, is one of the most popular lochs in the park. Surrounded by pine forests and overlooked by the Cairngorm Mountains, Loch Morlich is a stunning spot for water-based activities. The loch also has a sandy beach, which is a rare find in the Highlands and a popular spot for picnics and sunbathing.

River Spey: The River Spey, one of Scotland's longest and most famous rivers, flows through the Cairngorms National Park. The river is renowned for its salmon fishing and is also a popular route for canoeing and kayaking. The Speyside Way, a long-distance walking trail, follows the course of the river and offers a scenic route through the park.

Winter in the Cairngorms: A Snowy Wonderland

Cairngorms National Park is also a winter wonderland, offering some of the best skiing and snowboarding in the UK. The Cairngorm Mountain Resort, located near Aviemore, is a popular destination for winter sports enthusiasts, with a range of slopes suitable for all skill levels.

Skiing and Snowboarding: The resort offers a variety of runs, from gentle beginner slopes to challenging off-piste routes. The ski season typically runs from December to April, and the resort is equipped with lifts, rental shops, and a ski school.

Winter Wildlife: Winter is also a great time for wildlife watching in the Cairngorms. As the snow blankets the landscape, species such as ptarmigans and mountain hares can be spotted in their winter coats, blending in with the snowy surroundings.

Fingal's Cave

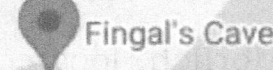

SCAN HERE

HOW TO USE QR CODE

- Open your phone's camera app or download scanner app from play store or apple store
- Point the camera at the QR code for a few seconds (no need to take a photo).
- A link should appear on the display, leading you to the location of the code

Cairngorms National Park

Cairngorms National Park

SCAN HERE

HOW TO USE QR CODE

- **Open your phone's camera app or download scanner app from play store or apple store**
- **Point the camera at the QR code for a few seconds (no need to take a photo).**
- **A link should appear on the display, leading you to the location of the code**

CHAPTER 5

SCOTTISH CULTURE AND TRADITIONS

Festivals and Events

Scotland is a land rich in history, tradition, and cultural expression, and this vibrant heritage is showcased through its numerous festivals and events. Throughout the year, Scotland hosts an array of celebrations that draw visitors from around the world, offering a unique insight into the nation's soul. From the world-famous Edinburgh Festival Fringe to the ancient customs of Hogmanay and the spirited competitions of the Highland Games, these events are not just entertainment—they are a living testament to Scotland's enduring cultural legacy.

Edinburgh Festival Fringe: The World's Largest Arts Festival

The Edinburgh Festival Fringe, often referred to simply as "the Fringe," is the largest and most celebrated arts festival in the world. Held annually in Scotland's capital during August, the Fringe transforms Edinburgh into a buzzing hub of creativity, drawing performers, artists, and audiences from every corner of the globe.

The Origins and Growth of the Fringe

The Edinburgh Festival Fringe began in 1947 when eight theatre groups turned up uninvited to perform at the inaugural Edinburgh International Festival, a more formal event focused on classical arts. These performers were "on the fringe" of the official event, hence the name. What started as an act of rebellion has since grown into an extraordinary celebration of the arts, where anyone with a story to tell and a stage to perform on is welcome.

Diversity of Performances: The Fringe is known for its eclectic mix of performances, which range from traditional theatre and dance to experimental art forms and avant-garde productions. Comedy is a particularly strong presence, with many comedians considering the Fringe as the ultimate testing ground for new material. However, the festival also showcases music, cabaret, circus acts, spoken word, and more.

The Venues: Edinburgh's historic and atmospheric venues add to the festival's charm. Performances take place in an astonishing variety of spaces, from grand theatres and concert halls to churches, pubs, and even street corners. The city itself becomes a stage, with impromptu performances and buskers adding to the vibrant atmosphere.

Navigating the Festival: With thousands of shows on offer, planning your Fringe experience can be overwhelming. The festival's official program is a hefty tome, and there are also apps and websites dedicated to helping you discover performances that suit your tastes. Some seasoned Fringe-goers recommend taking a chance on lesser-known acts or attending "pay what you can" shows, where the audience decides the price.

The Fringe Society and Its Role

The Fringe Society, established in 1958, plays a crucial role in supporting performers and audiences. It provides resources, advice, and a central hub for ticketing and information. The society operates under the principle that anyone can perform at the Fringe, maintaining the festival's open-access policy, which is key to its unique and democratic spirit.

Impact and Legacy

The Edinburgh Festival Fringe has had a profound impact on the global arts scene. It has launched the careers of countless artists, comedians, and playwrights, and its influence is felt far beyond Scotland. The festival has inspired similar events worldwide, but none rival the scale and prestige of the Edinburgh original. For visitors, attending the Fringe is an unforgettable experience, offering a deep dive into the creative heart of Scotland.

Hogmanay: Scotland's Legendary New Year's Celebration

Hogmanay, Scotland's New Year's Eve celebration, is one of the most anticipated and lively events on the Scottish calendar. While New Year's Eve is celebrated worldwide, Hogmanay in Scotland is something truly special, steeped in tradition, ritual, and a bit of mystery.

The Origins of Hogmanay

The exact origins of Hogmanay are unclear, but it is believed to have roots in ancient winter solstice festivals, possibly influenced by the Viking celebration of Yule. The name "Hogmanay" itself is thought to derive from a variety of sources, including French and Norse words related to feasting and gift-giving. Over time, these influences blended with Scottish customs to create a unique celebration that marks the end of the old year and the beginning of the new.

First-Footing: One of the most cherished Hogmanay traditions is "first-footing," where the first person to enter your home after midnight is believed to bring good luck for the coming year. Traditionally, this visitor should be a tall, dark-haired man, and he should carry symbolic gifts such as coal (for warmth), shortbread (for food), and whisky (for good cheer).

The Bells: The moment the clock strikes midnight is known as "the bells," and it is met with a chorus of "Auld Lang Syne," the famous song by Scotland's national poet, Robert Burns. This emotional moment is often shared with friends and family, and it marks the official start of the new year.

Fire Festivals and Torchlight Processions: Fire has long been a symbol of purification and renewal, and it plays a central role in many Hogmanay celebrations. In Edinburgh, the Torchlight Procession is a spectacular event that sees thousands of participants carrying flaming torches through the city streets, creating a river of fire that winds its way to Calton Hill for a dramatic finale of fireworks and music. Other towns, such as Stonehaven and Biggar, have their fire festivals, where traditions such as the swinging of fireballs and the burning of effigies are carried out to ward off evil spirits and welcome the new year.

Edinburgh's Hogmanay: A World-Famous Festival

Edinburgh's Hogmanay celebrations are among the most famous in the world, attracting visitors from far and wide. The city hosts a series of events over several days, culminating in the massive street party on

December 31st. The festivities include concerts, ceilidh dancing, and a spectacular fireworks display over Edinburgh Castle.

Street Party: The Hogmanay Street Party is a ticketed event that sees thousands of travellers gather in the heart of Edinburgh to celebrate. Multiple stages feature live music from top Scottish and international artists, while DJs keep the crowds dancing well into the night.

Loony Dook: For those looking to start the new year with a shock to the system, the Loony Dook is a New Year's Day tradition where participants take a plunge into the freezing waters of the Firth of Forth, often in fancy dress. This chilly dip is not for the faint-hearted but is a fun and invigorating way to kick off the year.

The Spirit of Hogmanay

Hogmanay is more than just a party; it's a reflection of Scotland's rich cultural heritage and a time for both celebration and reflection. Whether you're joining the crowds in Edinburgh or experiencing the festivities in a small village, Hogmanay offers a unique opportunity to connect with Scottish traditions and welcome the new year with joy and optimism.

Highland Games: Celebrating Scotland's Strength and Heritage

The Highland Games are a series of traditional Scottish events held throughout the country, particularly during the summer months. These gatherings celebrate Scottish and Celtic culture, featuring athletic competitions, music, dancing, and displays of strength and endurance. The Highland Games are a vibrant expression of Scottish heritage, and they attract both locals and tourists who come to witness the spectacle and take part in the festivities.

The Origins of the Highland Games

The history of the Highland Games is shrouded in legend and tradition. Some believe the games date back to the 11th century when King Malcolm III of Scotland summoned men to race up Craig Choinnich as part of a contest to find the fastest runner to serve as his royal messenger. Others trace the games' origins to the clan gatherings, where rival clans would compete in tests of strength and skill.

The Events of the Highland Games

The Highland Games feature a variety of events, some of which are unique to Scotland and reflect the country's rugged landscape and warrior spirit.

Caber Toss: Perhaps the most iconic of all Highland Games events, the caber toss involves competitors lifting and flipping a large wooden log (the caber) end over end. The goal is not just to toss the caber but to do so with precision, ideally causing it to land in a straight line away from the thrower.

Stone Put: Similar to the shot put, the stone put involves throwing a large stone as far as possible. This event highlights the strength and technique of the athletes.

Hammer Throw: In the hammer throw, competitors swing a heavy weight attached to a long handle before releasing it into the air. The hammer must be thrown with power and control, and the longest throw wins.

Tug of War: The tug of war is a team event that pits groups against each other in a test of strength and endurance. The sight of teams straining and pulling against each other is a classic image of the Highland Games.

Music and Dance

No Highland Games would be complete without the stirring sound of bagpipes and the grace of traditional Scottish dance. Piping competitions are a staple of the games, with bands competing in categories that showcase their skill and precision. The highland dance, often performed in traditional attire, is another highlight, with dancers demonstrating agility and grace in a series of intricate steps and movements.

Clan Gatherings

The Highland Games are also an opportunity for clan members to gather and celebrate their shared heritage. Many games include a clan village, where attendees can learn about Scotland's clans, explore their genealogy, and connect with their ancestral roots. This sense of community and pride in one's heritage is a central aspect of the Highland Games.

Where to Experience the Highland Games

The Highland Games are held across Scotland, with some of the most famous events taking place in Braemar, Oban, and Inverness. The Braemar Gathering, attended by members of the British royal family, is one of the most prestigious and draws visitors from around the world. Whether you attend a large gathering or a smaller, local event, the Highland Games offer an authentic and memorable Scottish experience.

Cuisine and Dining

Scotland's culinary scene is a reflection of its rich history, diverse landscapes, and deep-rooted traditions. From hearty, rustic dishes that have sustained Scots for centuries to innovative cuisine that blends local ingredients with global influences, Scottish food offers a wide array of flavours and experiences. In this section, we will explore the must-try dishes that define Scottish cuisine, delve into the world of Scotch whisky, and guide you to the best restaurants and local markets where you can savour the authentic taste of Scotland.

Must-Try Scottish Dishes

Scottish cuisine is a celebration of the land and sea, with dishes that often highlight the country's natural bounty. Here are some iconic Scottish foods that you simply must try during your visit.

Haggis: Scotland's National Dish

No exploration of Scottish cuisine would be complete without mentioning haggis, the country's national dish. Haggis is a savoury pudding made from sheep's offal (heart, liver, and lungs), minced with onion, oatmeal, suet, and spices, and traditionally encased in the animal's stomach. While the ingredients might seem unusual to the uninitiated, haggis has a rich, earthy flavour and a satisfying texture that has won over countless visitors.

Serving Suggestion: Haggis is typically served with "neeps and tatties" (mashed turnips and potatoes) and a whisky sauce. This dish is especially popular during Burns Night, a celebration held every January

25th in honour of Scotland's national poet, Robert Burns, who famously penned an ode to haggis.

Scottish Seafood: Fresh from the Cold Waters

Scotland's long coastline and abundant rivers and lochs make it a paradise for seafood lovers. The country is renowned for its fresh, high-quality seafood, with specialities that include salmon, scallops, oysters, and langoustines.

Smoked Salmon: Scottish smoked salmon is prized worldwide for its delicate, rich flavour. The fish is cured and cold-smoked to create a product that is both luxurious and versatile. Whether enjoyed on its own, with scrambled eggs or as part of a more elaborate dish, Scottish smoked salmon is a true delicacy.

Cullen Skink: This traditional Scottish soup is a comforting dish made with smoked haddock, potatoes, onions, and milk or cream. Cullen skink is a favourite in the colder months and is often served as a starter in Scottish homes and restaurants.

Black Pudding: A Hearty Breakfast Staple

Black pudding is a type of blood sausage made from pork or beef blood, oatmeal, and seasoning. It has a distinctive flavour that is both savoury and slightly sweet, with a dense texture that makes it a filling and satisfying meal.

Serving Suggestion: Black pudding is a staple of the traditional Scottish breakfast, often served alongside eggs, bacon, sausage, baked beans, and toast. It can also be enjoyed as part of a more refined dish, paired with scallops or incorporated into a rich, flavourful salad.

Shortbread: A Sweet Treat with a Scottish Twist

Shortbread is one of Scotland's most famous exports, known for its rich, buttery flavour and crumbly texture. This simple yet delicious biscuit is made from flour, butter, and sugar, and it has been enjoyed in Scotland for centuries.

Variations: While traditional shortbread is always a treat, you'll also find variations that incorporate flavours like lavender, lemon, or chocolate.

It's the perfect accompaniment to a cup of tea or coffee, and a popular souvenir to bring home.

Scotch Whisky: The Water of Life

Scotch whisky, often simply referred to as "Scotch," is perhaps Scotland's most famous export. This iconic spirit has been produced in Scotland for centuries, with a heritage that is deeply intertwined with the country's history and culture.

The Distillation Process

Scotch whisky is made from malted barley (in the case of single malt whisky) or other grains (for blended whisky), which are mashed, fermented, distilled, and aged in oak barrels. The ageing process, which must last at least three years by law, is what gives Scotch its complex flavours and characteristics.

Single Malt vs. Blended Whisky: Single malt Scotch whisky is produced at a single distillery using only malted barley, while blended Scotch whisky is a mix of whiskies from different distilleries, including both malt and grain whiskies. Each type has its unique appeal, with single malts often prized for their purity of flavour and complexity, and blended whiskies appreciated for their smoothness and balance.

Scotch Whisky Regions

Scotland is divided into several whisky-producing regions, each with its distinctive style:

Speyside: Known for its rich, sweet whiskies, often with notes of apple, pear, honey, and vanilla. Speyside is home to some of the most famous distilleries, including Glenfiddich and Macallan.

Islay: Famous for its peaty, smoky whiskies that often carry flavours of the sea, such as Laphroaig and Ardbeg. Islay whiskies are bold and intense, beloved by aficionados of strong, distinctive spirits.

Highlands: The largest whisky-producing region, offering a diverse range of styles. Highland whiskies can be rich and full-bodied or light and floral, depending on the distillery. Glenmorangie and Oban are well-known examples.

Lowlands: Known for their lighter, more delicate whiskies, often with grassy, citrusy notes. Lowland whiskies are ideal for those new to Scotch or those who prefer a subtler, more refined flavour.

Campbeltown: Once a major whisky-producing region, Campbeltown now has only a few distilleries, but the whiskies are known for their complexity, with a maritime influence and a balance of sweetness and smoke.

Whisky Tasting and Distillery Tours

One of the best ways to experience Scotch whisky is by visiting a distillery. Many distilleries across Scotland offer tours that take you through the whisky-making process, from malting and mashing to distillation and ageing. These tours usually end with a tasting session, where you can sample the distillery's products and gain a deeper appreciation for the nuances of Scotch whisky.

Top Restaurants and Local Markets in Scotland

Scotland's dining scene is a vibrant mix of traditional and contemporary, with an emphasis on fresh, local ingredients. From Michelin-starred restaurants to bustling local markets, here's where to find the best of Scottish cuisine.

Top Restaurants

The Kitchin (Edinburgh): Located in the heart of Edinburgh, The Kitchin is a Michelin-starred restaurant that offers a modern take on traditional Scottish cuisine. Chef Tom Kitchin's "from nature to plate" philosophy is evident in every dish, with a focus on seasonal, locally sourced ingredients.

Ubiquitous Chip (Glasgow): A Glasgow institution, Ubiquitous Chip has been serving up Scottish cuisine with a creative twist for over 40 years. The menu features dishes like venison haggis and roast lamb, all served in a charming, plant-filled dining room.

Loch Fyne Restaurant (Cairndow, Argyll): For seafood lovers, Loch Fyne Restaurant is a must-visit. Situated on the shores of Loch Fyne, this restaurant specializes in fresh, sustainably sourced seafood, including oysters, mussels, and smoked salmon.

Local Markets

Edinburgh Farmers' Market: Held every Saturday on Castle Terrace, this market offers a wide range of local produce, from fresh vegetables and fruits to artisanal cheeses, meats, and baked goods. It's the perfect place to pick up ingredients for a picnic or to sample some of Scotland's best food.

Glasgow's Barras Market: A historic market in the East End of Glasgow, the Barras Market is a lively and eclectic mix of stalls selling everything from antiques and clothing to fresh produce and street food. It's a great spot to soak up the local atmosphere and grab a bite to eat.

Inverness Victorian Market: Located in the heart of Inverness, this charming covered market is home to a variety of independent vendors offering everything from fresh fish and meats to handmade crafts and souvenirs. It's a wonderful place to explore local flavours and find unique gifts.

Music and Dance

Scotland's cultural identity is deeply intertwined with its music and dance, both of which have played vital roles in the lives of Scots for centuries. From the haunting strains of the bagpipes echoing through the glens to the lively rhythms of folk songs and the spirited movements of traditional dances, music and dance are more than just forms of entertainment in Scotland—they are a living link to the past and a vibrant expression of national pride.

we will explore the rich traditions of Scottish music, delve into the significance of dance in Scottish culture, and discover how these art forms continue to thrive in the modern era. Whether you're a visitor eager to immerse yourself in Scottish culture or simply curious about the sounds and movements that define this remarkable country, this guide will provide a comprehensive overview of Scotland's musical and dance heritage.

The Bagpipes: Scotland's Iconic Instrument

When one thinks of Scottish music, the bagpipes are often the first instrument that comes to mind. This unique and powerful instrument has become a symbol of Scotland, recognised around the world for its distinctive sound.

Origins and History

The bagpipes have a long and storied history, with variations of the instrument found in many cultures worldwide. However, as it is known today, the Great Highland Bagpipe is the version most closely associated with Scotland. The exact origins of the bagpipes in Scotland are unclear, but they are believed to have been brought to the country by the Romans or the Celts. By the Middle Ages, the bagpipes had become an integral part of Scottish culture, used in both civilian and military life.

The Structure of the Bagpipes

The Great Highland Bagpipe consists of several key components:

The Bag: Made from animal hide or synthetic materials, the bag is filled with air by the piper and serves as the reservoir that provides a steady supply of air to the pipes.

The Chanter: The chanter is the melody pipe that produces the notes. It has a range of nine notes and is played with both hands.

The Drones: The bagpipes typically have three drones—two tenor drones and one bass drone—that produce a continuous harmonic background to the melody. The drones are tuned to the same pitch, creating the iconic drone sound associated with the instrument.

The Blowpipe: The blowpipe is used to inflate the bag with air, either by mouth or with a bellows.

The Role of Bagpipes in Scottish Culture

Throughout history, the bagpipes have played a significant role in Scottish culture, particularly in military and ceremonial contexts. In battle, the sound of the pipes was used to rally troops, intimidate the enemy, and communicate orders. The bagpipes were also a fixture at clan gatherings, weddings, funerals, and other important events.

Today, the bagpipes continue to be a powerful symbol of Scotland, often heard at national celebrations, parades, and Highland Games. Many pipers take pride in their craft, and pipe bands—groups of pipers and drummers—are a common sight at festivals and competitions both in Scotland and abroad.

Learning to Play the Bagpipes

For those interested in learning to play the bagpipes, there are numerous resources available, including schools, workshops, and online tutorials. Mastering the bagpipes requires dedication and practice, but it offers a rewarding connection to Scotland's musical heritage. Whether you're a beginner or an experienced musician, playing the bagpipes is a deeply satisfying way to engage with Scottish culture.

Folk Music: The Soul of Scotland

While the bagpipes may be the most iconic of Scottish instruments, Scotland's folk music tradition is equally rich and diverse. Folk songs have been passed down through generations, telling the stories of Scotland's people, their struggles, joys, and the beauty of the land they call home.

Traditional Instruments

In addition to the bagpipes, Scottish folk music features a variety of traditional instruments, each contributing to the distinctive sound of the genre:

The Fiddle: The Scottish fiddle is similar to the violin but is played in a style that is unique to Scottish folk music. Fiddle tunes are often lively and rhythmic, with a strong emphasis on melody and ornamentation. The fiddle has been a central instrument in Scottish folk music for centuries and remains popular today.

The Accordion: The accordion, with its rich, resonant sound, is another key instrument in Scottish folk music. It is often used to accompany dances and songs, adding depth and texture to the music.

The Clàrsach (Scottish Harp): The clàrsach is a small Celtic harp with a history that dates back over a thousand years. Its delicate, ethereal sound is often associated with the Highlands and Islands, and it has experienced a revival in recent years, with many contemporary musicians exploring its potential.

The Tin Whistle and Flute: These wind instruments are also commonly found in Scottish folk music. The tin whistle, with its bright, piercing tone, is often used in lively dance tunes, while the wooden flute offers a more mellow, expressive sound.

Folk Songs and Ballads

Scottish folk music is renowned for its ballads—narrative songs that tell stories of love, war, betrayal, and adventure. These songs often draw on historical events, local legends, and the natural landscape, creating a deep sense of place and identity.

"The Skye Boat Song": One of the most famous Scottish folk songs, "The Skye Boat Song" tells the story of Bonnie Prince Charlie's escape to the Isle of Skye after the Battle of Culloden in 1746. The song's haunting melody and poignant lyrics have made it a beloved classic, often performed by both traditional and contemporary artists.

"Auld Lang Syne": Written by Scotland's national poet, Robert Burns, "Auld Lang Syne" is perhaps the most widely recognized Scottish song. Traditionally sung at the stroke of midnight on New Year's Eve, the song is a reflection on old friendships and the passage of time.

"Loch Lomond": This popular ballad, with its refrain "You take the high road, and I'll take the low road," is a love song that has become an anthem for Scottish pride and nostalgia. The song's origins are unclear, but it is often associated with the Jacobite uprisings.

Folk Music in Modern Scotland

While deeply rooted in tradition, Scottish folk music is also a living, evolving art form. Today, many musicians are blending traditional sounds with contemporary influences, creating a vibrant and dynamic folk scene. Festivals like Celtic Connections in Glasgow and the

Edinburgh Folk Festival celebrate this diversity, showcasing both established and emerging artists.

Scottish Dance: A Celebration of Community and Tradition

Dance is an integral part of Scottish culture, with a variety of traditional dances that have been enjoyed for centuries. These dances are often performed at social gatherings, weddings, and festivals, bringing people together in a joyful celebration of community and heritage.

Highland Dancing

Highland dancing is one of the most iconic forms of Scottish dance, known for its athleticism, precision, and grace. Traditionally performed by men, Highland dancing is now enjoyed by both men and women and is often seen at the Highland Games and other cultural events.

The Sword Dance: One of the oldest and most famous Highland dances, the Sword Dance involves intricate footwork around a pair of crossed swords. The dance is said to have originated on the battlefield, where warriors would perform it before going into battle, believing that completing the dance would bring them victory.

The Highland Fling: Another popular Highland dance, the Highland Fling is a solo dance that showcases the dancer's agility and stamina. The dance is performed on the spot, with the dancer executing a series of precise movements and leaps.

Ceilidh Dancing

Ceilidh dancing (pronounced "kay-lee") is a social form of dancing that is deeply embedded in Scottish culture. A ceilidh is a traditional Scottish gathering that features music, dancing, and storytelling, and it remains a popular form of entertainment at weddings, parties, and community events.

The Gay Gordons: One of the most well-known ceilidh dances, the Gay Gordons is a simple yet lively dance that is often used to start a ceilidh. It involves pairs of dancers moving in a circle, switching partners, and performing a series of steps to a lively tune.

The Dashing White Sergeant: This dance is performed in groups of six, with three people on each side. The dancers move in a series of circles and figure-of-eight patterns, accompanied by a lively reel.

Strip the Willow: A high-energy dance that is a staple of any ceilidh, Strip the Willow involves long lines of dancers who weave in and out of each other, spinning their partners as they go. It's a fast-paced and fun dance that often leaves participants breathless and smiling.

Dance in Modern Scotland

While traditional dances like Highland and ceilidh dancing remain popular, Scotland's dance scene is also embracing contemporary styles. Scottish Ballet, the national ballet company, and various modern dance troupes are pushing the boundaries of dance, blending traditional techniques with innovative choreography.

Crafts and Souvenirs

Scotland is a country rich in history, culture, and craftsmanship, where tradition and creativity blend seamlessly to produce some of the world's most cherished and distinctive crafts. From the iconic tartan patterns to the luxurious Harris Tweed, Scottish crafts are not only a testament to the country's skilled artisans but also a tangible link to its storied past.

we'll delve into the world of authentic Scottish crafts, exploring the origins and significance of these traditional items, and offering tips on where to find the highest-quality souvenirs. Whether you're looking to bring home a piece of Scotland's heritage or searching for the perfect gift, this guide will help you navigate the vast array of Scottish crafts with confidence.

Tartan: The Symbol of Scottish Identity

Few things are as synonymous with Scotland as tartan. This distinctive checkered pattern, with its bold colours and intricate designs, is more than just fabric—it's a powerful symbol of Scottish identity and heritage.

History and Significance

Tartan has a long and fascinating history that is closely intertwined with Scotland's clans. Originally, tartan patterns, or "setts," were associated with specific regions or families, and wearing a particular tartan was a way of signifying one's allegiance to a clan. Each clan had its unique tartan, and the colours and patterns often held symbolic meanings, such as the natural dyes available in the area or the clan's historical alliances.

During the 18th century, following the Jacobite uprisings, the wearing of tartan was banned by the British government in an attempt to suppress Highland culture. However, this ban was lifted in 1782, and Tartan experienced a resurgence, becoming a symbol of Scottish pride and resistance. Today, tartan is worn with pride by Scots around the world and is a central feature of traditional Scottish attire, such as the kilt.

Types of Tartan

There are thousands of different tartans, each with its unique design and story. Some of the most well-known types include:

Clan Tartans: These are the traditional tartans associated with specific Scottish clans. If you have Scottish ancestry, you may be able to trace your heritage to a particular clan and find the tartan that represents your family's history.

District Tartans: These tartans are associated with particular regions or districts in Scotland. Even if you don't belong to a Scottish clan, you can wear a district tartan to show your connection to a particular area of Scotland.

Royal Tartans: These tartans are reserved for the British royal family and include the Royal Stewart and the Balmoral tartans. While some royal tartans are restricted, others, like the Royal Stewart, are widely available and popular.

Fashion Tartans: In recent years, tartan has become a popular fashion statement, with designers creating modern interpretations of traditional patterns. These tartans may not be associated with a specific clan or region, but they offer a contemporary way to embrace this iconic fabric.

Where to Buy Tartan

When shopping for tartan, it's important to seek out high-quality, authentic products. Scotland is home to numerous reputable weavers and tailors who produce beautiful tartan garments and accessories. Here are a few recommendations:

House of Edgar (Perth): One of Scotland's most famous tartan manufacturers, House of Edgar offers a wide range of clan and fashion tartans, all woven from the finest materials.

Lochcarron of Scotland (Selkirk): With a history dating back to 1892, Lochcarron is renowned for its extensive collection of tartans and is a popular choice for those looking to purchase kilts, scarves, and other tartan products.

Kinloch Anderson (Edinburgh): A royal warrant holder, Kinloch Anderson has been making kilts and other traditional Scottish garments since 1868. Their products are known for their exceptional craftsmanship and attention to detail.

The Tartan Weaving Mill (Edinburgh): Located on the Royal Mile, this shop offers visitors the chance to see tartan being woven on traditional looms. It's a great place to learn about the history of tartan and purchase authentic products.

Harris Tweed: The Fabric of the Hebrides

Harris Tweed is another iconic Scottish fabric, renowned for its quality, durability, and timeless style. Handwoven by islanders in the Outer Hebrides, Harris Tweed is a true product of its environment, reflecting the rugged beauty of the Scottish landscape.

The Origins of Harris Tweed

The story of Harris Tweed begins on the Isle of Harris, where the fabric has been woven by hand for centuries. Originally, tweed was made by crofters for their use, using wool from local sheep that was dyed with natural plant dyes. The distinctive patterns and colours of Harris Tweed were inspired by the landscape, with earthy tones reflecting the heather-covered hills and vibrant blues and greens echoing the sea and sky.

In the 19th century, Lady Dunmore, the widow of the Earl of Dunmore, recognized the potential of Harris Tweed as a commercial product. She began promoting the fabric to her wealthy friends in London, and its popularity quickly grew. Today, Harris Tweed is a globally recognized brand, protected by law under the Harris Tweed Act of 1993, which ensures that all Harris Tweed is handwoven in the Outer Hebrides.

Characteristics of Harris Tweed

What sets Harris Tweed apart from other fabrics is its unique production process. Each length of Harris Tweed is:

Handwoven: By law, Harris Tweed must be woven by hand at the home of the weaver, using traditional looms. This gives the fabric its distinctive texture and character.

Made from Pure Virgin Wool: The wool used in Harris Tweed is sourced from sheep raised in the Outer Hebrides and the Scottish mainland. The wool is carefully dyed, blended, carded, spun, warped, and woven to create the final product.

Durable and Weather-Resistant: Harris Tweed is known for its durability and ability to withstand harsh weather conditions, making it ideal for outdoor wear. The fabric is tightly woven, which helps to repel water and retain heat.

Where to Buy Harris Tweed

If you're looking to purchase authentic Harris Tweed, there are several places to consider:

Harris Tweed Hebrides (Isle of Harris): This company is one of the largest producers of Harris Tweed and offers a wide range of products, from traditional jackets and caps to modern accessories like bags and wallets.

Harris Tweed Authority (Stornoway): The Harris Tweed Authority oversees the production of Harris Tweed and ensures that all products meet the strict legal requirements. Their website offers information on where to buy genuine Harris Tweed items.

MacLeod & MacLeod (Stornoway): A family-run business with a long history in the Harris Tweed industry, MacLeod & MacLeod is known for its high-quality garments and accessories.

Highland House of Fraser (Inverness): This well-known Highland retailer offers a range of Harris Tweed products, including jackets, hats, and scarves, all made from the finest tweed.

Scottish Jewelry: A Tradition of Craftsmanship

Scotland has a long tradition of jewellery-making, with designs that are often inspired by the country's rich history and natural beauty. From delicate Celtic knotwork to bold, modern creations, Scottish jewellery is renowned for its craftsmanship and artistry.

Celtic Jewelry

Celtic designs are a common theme in Scottish jewellery, with intricate patterns that often feature knots, spirals, and other symbols. These designs have deep roots in Scottish history, dating back to the ancient Celts who inhabited the British Isles.

Celtic Knots: These endless loops, with no beginning or end, are a symbol of eternity and interconnectedness. They are often used in rings, necklaces, and bracelets.

Trinity Knot (Triquetra): The trinity knot is another popular motif, symbolizing the Holy Trinity in Christianity or the three elements of nature—earth, air, and water—in Celtic tradition.

Claddagh: Though originally an Irish symbol, the Claddagh has also become popular in Scotland. The design features two hands holding a heart, often topped with a crown, representing love, loyalty, and friendship.

Heather Gem Jewelry

Heather gem jewellery is a unique Scottish craft, made from the stems of heather plants that grow in the Highlands. The stems are gathered, dyed in vibrant colours, and compressed to create a material that is then cut and polished into gemstones. These colourful stones are set in silver or gold to create beautiful brooches, pendants, earrings, and more.

Where to Buy Scottish Jewelry

For those looking to purchase authentic Scottish jewellery, here are a few top recommendations:

Hamilton & Inches (Edinburgh): This prestigious jeweller has been crafting exquisite pieces since 1866 and holds a royal warrant. Their collection includes both traditional and contemporary designs.

Celtic Art (Inverness): Specializing in Celtic and Pictish designs, Celtic Art offers a wide range of handcrafted jewellery that celebrates Scotland's ancient heritage.

Ortak (Kirkwall, Orkney): Known for its beautiful silver and gold jewellery, Ortak's designs often draw inspiration from the natural world and Scotland's history.

Sheila Fleet (Orkney): One of Scotland's leading jewellery designers, Sheila Fleet creates stunning pieces that reflect the landscapes and legends of the Orkney Islands.

Where to Find Quality Souvenirs

When it comes to buying souvenirs in Scotland, it's important to seek out authentic, high-quality items. Here are a few tips on where to find the best Scottish crafts and souvenirs:

Local Craft Fairs and Markets: Scotland hosts numerous craft fairs and markets throughout the year, where you can find handmade items from local artisans. Look for events like the Edinburgh Christmas Market, the Highland Games, or the Royal Highland Show.

Artisan Shops and Studios: Many towns and cities in Scotland have artisan shops and studios where you can purchase directly from the maker. These shops often offer a wide range of crafts, including pottery, textiles, and jewellery.

Heritage Centres and Museums: Heritage centres and museums often have gift shops that sell high-quality, authentic Scottish crafts. These locations are also great places to learn more about the history and significance of the items you're purchasing.

Online Stores: If you're unable to visit Scotland in person, many Scottish artisans and retailers have online stores where you can browse and purchase their products. Websites like Scottish Fine Soaps, Harris Tweed Authority, and Celtic & Co offer a wide selection of traditional crafts.

Crafts and Souvenirs

When you visit Scotland, the experience isn't complete without taking a piece of the country home with you. Whether you're a first-time visitor or someone who's fallen in love with Scotland over multiple trips, the country's crafts and souvenirs offer a tangible connection to its rich heritage, culture, and artistry. From the iconic tartan patterns to the luxurious texture of Harris Tweed and the intricate designs of Celtic jewellery, Scotland's crafts are a testament to the skills passed down through generations. This guide will help you navigate the world of Scottish crafts and souvenirs, ensuring you bring home something truly authentic.

Tartan: A Symbol of Scottish Heritage

Tartan is perhaps the most recognizable symbol of Scotland. These patterned cloths, consisting of crisscrossed horizontal and vertical bands in multiple colours, are more than just fabric; they represent the clans, history, and identity of Scotland. Each tartan pattern is associated with a specific clan, region, or family, making it a deeply personal and meaningful item.

The History of Tartan

Tartan has been worn in Scotland for centuries, with its origins dating back to at least the 3rd century AD. Historically, tartans were made from wool dyed with natural plant and animal dyes, creating distinct patterns unique to specific regions. By the 16th century, tartan had become a symbol of Scottish clans, with different patterns, or "setts," representing different families or districts.

During the 18th century, after the Jacobite uprising, the British government banned the wearing of tartan through the Dress Act of 1746 in an attempt to suppress Highland culture. However, the ban was lifted in 1782, and Tartan experienced a resurgence, eventually becoming a symbol of Scottish pride and identity.

Choosing Your Tartan

When purchasing tartan, consider whether you want to choose a pattern associated with your own family or clan. Even if you don't have Scottish heritage, you can still find a tartan that resonates with you—many patterns represent regions, organizations, or causes. For example, the Royal Stewart Tartan is associated with the royal family, while the Black Watch Tartan is linked to Scotland's military history.

Tartan items range from scarves and kilts to blankets, ties, and even handbags. Whether you choose a small accessory or a full traditional outfit, tartan is a timeless reminder of Scotland's enduring spirit.

Harris Tweed: The Fabric of the Isles

Harris Tweed is another iconic Scottish textile, known for its durability, warmth, and rich history. Produced exclusively in the Outer Hebrides, Harris Tweed is handwoven by local artisans using pure virgin wool. This wool is dyed and spun on the islands, giving Harris Tweed its unique character and connection to the rugged landscapes of Scotland.

The Origins of Harris Tweed

The production of Harris Tweed dates back to the early 19th century when the people of the Outer Hebrides began weaving cloth to keep warm in the harsh climate. Over time, Harris Tweed became highly sought after by the British aristocracy, particularly during the Victorian era, when it was used for everything from hunting jackets to upholstery.

The Harris Tweed Act of 1993 protects the name and ensures that only cloth woven in the Outer Hebrides can be labelled as Harris Tweed. This ensures that every piece of Harris Tweed is authentic and of the highest quality.

What to Buy in Harris Tweed

When shopping for Harris Tweed, you'll find a wide range of products, from traditional jackets and caps to modern accessories like handbags, wallets, and phone cases. Each item is marked with the Harris Tweed Orb, a symbol of authenticity that guarantees your purchase is genuine.

The versatility of Harris Tweed means it can be worn for both formal and casual occasions. Whether you're looking for a statement piece like a tailored jacket or a smaller item like a purse, Harris Tweed offers a piece of Scottish craftsmanship that will last for years to come.

Celtic Jewelry: Ancient Symbols and Modern Elegance

Celtic jewellery is another craft deeply embedded in Scotland's cultural heritage. Characterized by intricate knotwork, spirals, and symbolic designs, Celtic jewellery reflects the art and beliefs of Scotland's ancient peoples.

The Significance of Celtic Designs

Celtic designs are rich with symbolism. The iconic Celtic knot, for example, represents eternity and interconnectedness, with no beginning or end. Spirals often symbolize growth, life cycles, and the natural world, while other symbols like the Claddagh represent love, loyalty, and friendship.

These designs date back thousands of years and can be found in ancient stone carvings, manuscripts, and artefacts across Scotland. When you purchase a piece of Celtic jewellery, you're not just buying an accessory—you're acquiring a piece of history that carries deep cultural meaning.

Where to Find Authentic Celtic Jewelry

Scotland is home to many skilled jewellers who specialize in crafting Celtic designs. You can find beautiful pieces in gold, silver, and even gemstones, ranging from rings and necklaces to brooches and bracelets. Many jewellers use traditional methods to create their pieces, ensuring that each item is made with care and attention to detail.

Look for shops in cities like Edinburgh and Glasgow, as well as smaller towns and craft fairs. Some jewellers also offer custom designs, allowing you to create a unique piece that holds personal significance.

Whisky: A Taste of Scotland

While not a craft in the traditional sense, whisky is an essential part of Scotland's cultural heritage and makes for a popular souvenir. Scottish whisky, or Scotch, is renowned worldwide for its quality and distinctive flavours. Each region of Scotland produces whisky with its unique characteristics, from the smoky notes of Islay whiskies to the smooth, fruity flavours of those from Speyside.

Choosing the Right Whisky

When selecting a whisky to bring home, consider visiting a local distillery where you can learn about the production process and taste different varieties. Many distilleries offer tours and tastings, allowing you to find a whisky that suits your palate.

Bottles of whisky range from affordable everyday options to rare and collectable varieties. Whether you're a whisky connoisseur or simply want a taste of Scotland to enjoy at home, a bottle of Scotch makes for a memorable and enjoyable souvenir.

Where to Buy Quality Souvenirs

To ensure that you're bringing home authentic, high-quality items, here are a few tips on where to find the best Scottish crafts and souvenirs:

Local Craft Fairs and Markets: Scotland hosts numerous craft fairs and markets throughout the year, where you can find handmade items from local artisans. Look for events like the Edinburgh Christmas Market, the Highland Games, or the Royal Highland Show.

Artisan Shops and Studios: Many towns and cities in Scotland have artisan shops and studios where you can purchase directly from the maker. These shops often offer a wide range of crafts, including pottery, textiles, and jewellery.

Heritage Centres and Museums: Heritage centres and museums often have gift shops that sell high-quality, authentic Scottish crafts. These locations are also great places to learn more about the history and significance of the items you're purchasing.

Online Stores: If you're unable to visit Scotland in person, many Scottish artisans and retailers have online stores where you can browse and purchase their products. Websites like Scottish Fine Soaps, Harris Tweed Authority, and Celtic & Co offer a wide selection of traditional crafts.

The Kitchin (Edinburgh)

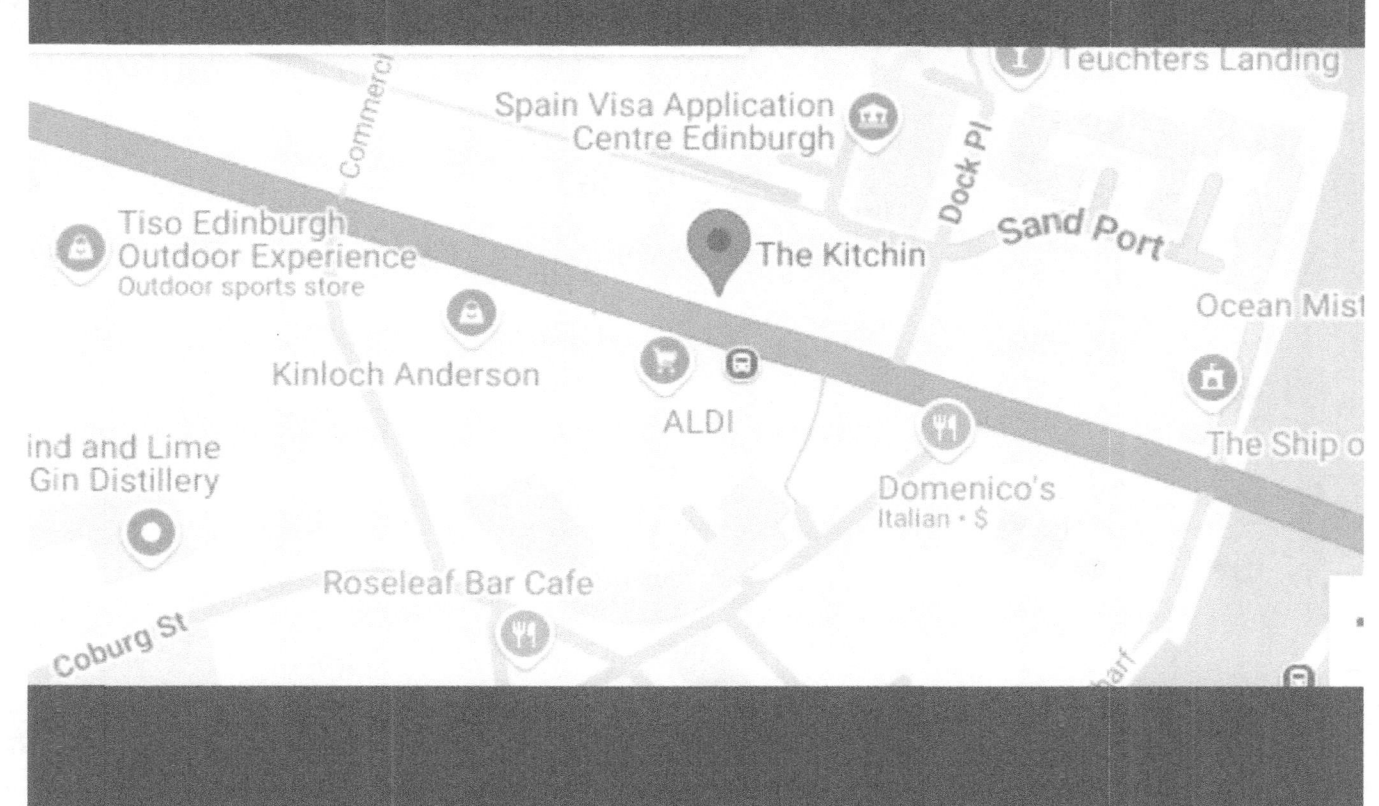

SCAN HERE

HOW TO USE QR CODE

- Open your phone's camera app or download scanner app from play store or apple store
- Point the camera at the QR code for a few seconds (no need to take a photo).
- A link should appear on the display, leading you to the location of the code

Ubiquitous Chip (Glasgow)

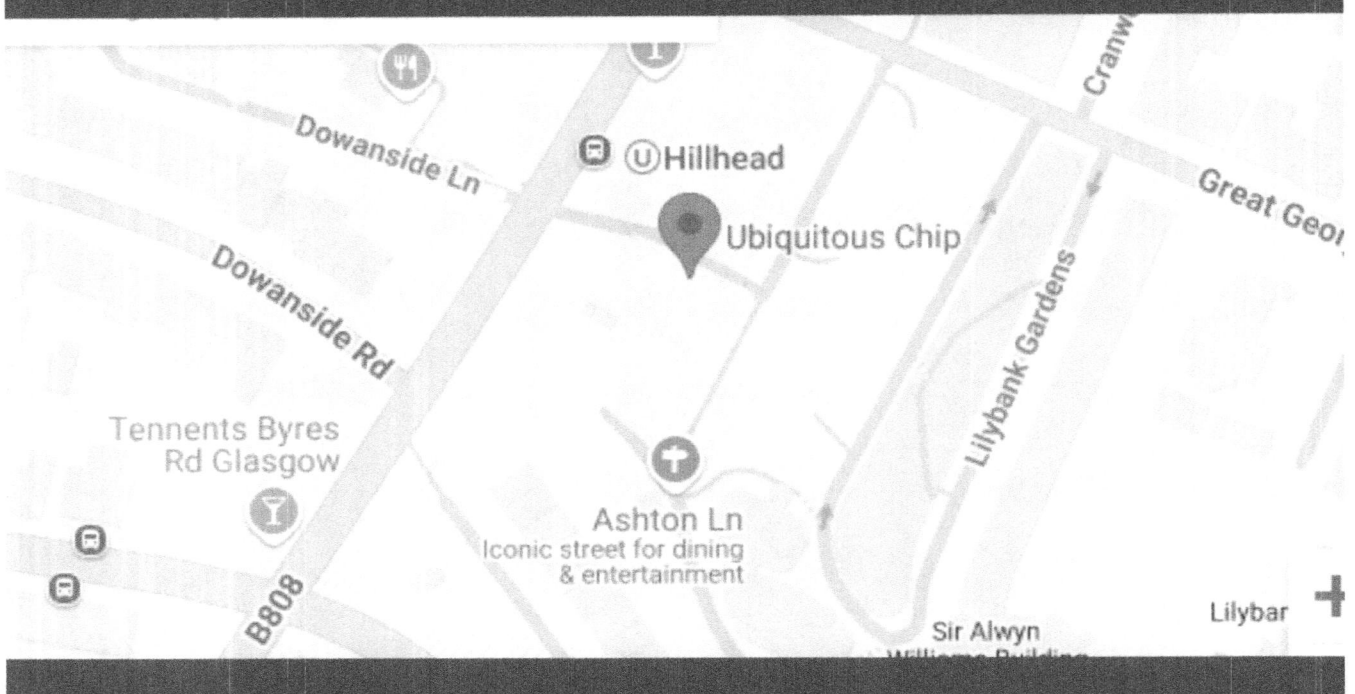

SCAN HERE

HOW TO USE QR CODE

- Open your phone's camera app or download scanner app from play store or apple store
- Point the camera at the QR code for a few seconds (no need to take a photo).
- A link should appear on the display, leading you to the location of the code

Loch Fyne Restaurant (Cairndow, Argyll)

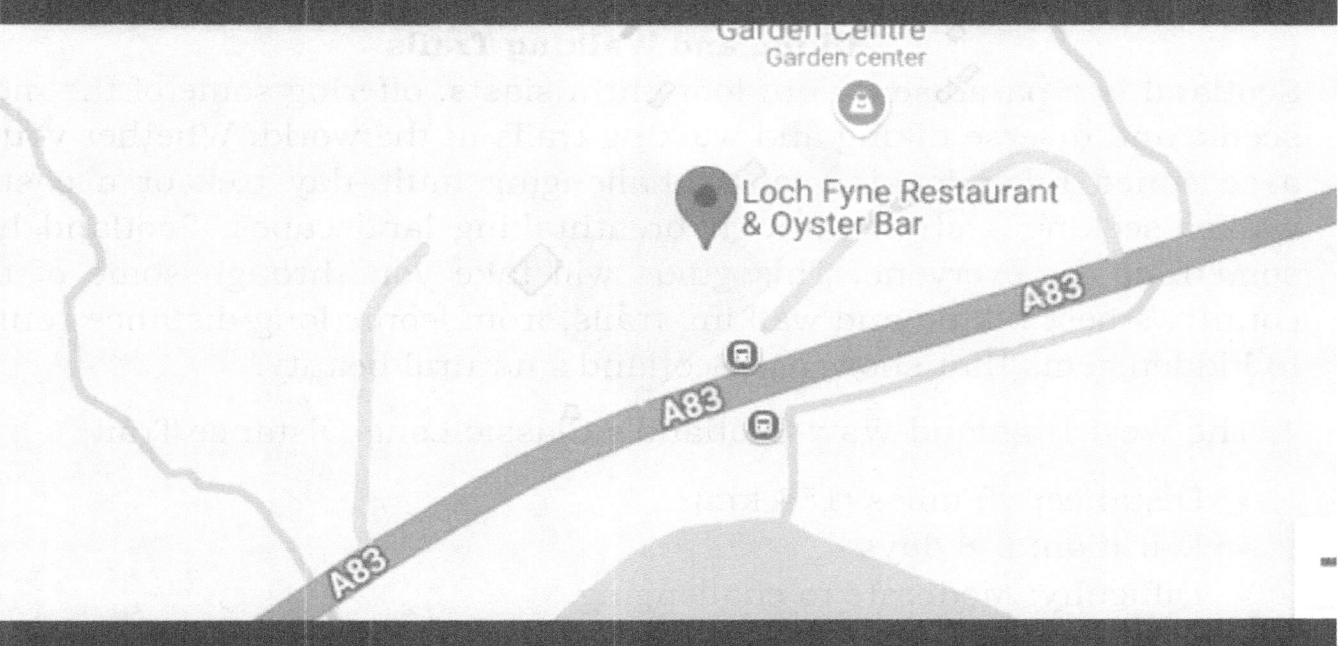

SCAN HERE

HOW TO USE QR CODE

- Open your phone's camera app or download scanner app from play store or apple store
- Point the camera at the QR code for a few seconds (no need to take a photo).
- A link should appear on the display, leading you to the location of the code

CHAPTER 6

OUTDOOR ADVENTURES

Hiking and Walking Trails

Scotland is a paradise for outdoor enthusiasts, offering some of the most scenic and diverse hiking and walking trails in the world. Whether you're a seasoned hiker looking for a challenging multi-day trek or a casual walker seeking a stroll through breathtaking landscapes, Scotland has something for everyone. This guide will take you through some of the country's best hiking and walking trails, from iconic long-distance routes to hidden gems that showcase Scotland's natural beauty.

1. The West Highland Way: Scotland's Classic Long-Distance Trail

- Distance: 96 miles (154 km)
- Duration: 6-8 days
- Difficulty: Moderate to challenging
- Starting Point: Milngavie, near Glasgow
- End Point: Fort William

The West Highland Way is Scotland's most famous long-distance trail, attracting hikers from around the world. This iconic route takes you through some of Scotland's most stunning landscapes, including Loch Lomond, Rannoch Moor, and the rugged mountains of the Highlands.

Highlights: The West Highland Way offers a diverse range of scenery, from tranquil lochside paths to remote moorlands and dramatic mountain views. Along the way, you'll pass through charming villages like Drymen and Tyndrum, and have the chance to explore historical sites such as the ruins of Inverlochy Castle.

Tips: The trail can be challenging in parts, especially the section over the Devil's Staircase, but it's well-marked and supported by accommodation options ranging from campsites to hotels. It's best to plan your trip and book accommodations early, especially during peak season.

2. The John Muir Way: A Journey Through Scotland's Heartland

- Distance: 134 miles (215 km)
- Duration: 7-10 days
- Difficulty: Moderate
- Starting Point: Helensburgh
- End Point: Dunbar

Named after the Scottish-American conservationist John Muir, this trail offers a unique blend of coastal and countryside walking. Stretching across Scotland from coast to coast, the John Muir Way takes you through a mix of urban areas, rural landscapes, and historic sites.

Highlights: The John Muir Way offers a varied experience, from the coastal beauty of the Firth of Clyde to the rolling hills of the Scottish Borders. Key sights include the Antonine Wall, Linlithgow Palace, and the picturesque town of North Berwick.

Tips: The trail is well-suited for both walking and cycling, and it's possible to tackle it in shorter sections if you don't have time for the full route. Be sure to explore the rich history along the way, as the trail passes many sites of cultural significance.

3. The Great Glen Way: From Coast to Coast Through the Highlands

- Distance: 79 miles (127 km)
- Duration: 5-7 days
- Difficulty: Moderate
- Starting Point: Fort William
- End Point: Inverness

The Great Glen Way follows the natural fault line that runs through the Highlands, connecting the west coast to the east coast of Scotland. This scenic trail takes you along the shores of famous lochs, including Loch Ness, and offers stunning views of the surrounding mountains.

Highlights: The Great Glen Way provides a more gentle hiking experience compared to some of Scotland's more rugged trails. Along the way, you'll enjoy panoramic views of Loch Ness, visit the historic town of

Fort Augustus, and have the chance to spot wildlife such as red deer and golden eagles.

Tips: The trail can be completed on foot or by bike, and there are options for shorter day hikes if you prefer not to tackle the entire route. Be sure to keep your camera ready for potential sightings of the elusive Loch Ness Monster!

4. The Southern Upland Way: Scotland's Longest Great Trail

- Distance: 214 miles (344 km)
- Duration: 12-16 days
- Difficulty: Challenging
- Starting Point: Portpatrick
- End Point: Cockburnspath

For those seeking a true challenge, the Southern Upland Way offers Scotland's longest continuous trail, crossing the country from coast to coast through the Southern Uplands. This demanding route takes you through some of Scotland's most remote and wild landscapes, offering a sense of solitude and adventure.

Highlights: The Southern Upland Way is known for its remote beauty, with vast moorlands, rolling hills, and dramatic coastlines. Along the way, you'll pass through historic towns like Moffat and Melrose, and encounter ancient monuments such as the Covenanters' Memorial.

Tips: This trail is best suited for experienced hikers, as it includes some strenuous sections and remote areas with limited facilities. Be prepared for varying weather conditions and plan your trip carefully, especially in terms of accommodation and supplies.

5. The Isle of Skye: The Quiraing and the Old Man of Storr

- Quiraing Circuit:
- Distance: 4.5 miles (7 km)
- Duration: 2-3 hours

- Difficulty: Moderate
- Old Man of Storr:
- Distance: 2.8 miles (4.5 km)
- Duration: 1.5-2 hours
- Difficulty: Moderate

The Isle of Skye is a hiker's dream, offering some of the most dramatic landscapes in Scotland. Two of the island's most famous walks are the Quiraing Circuit and the Old Man of Storr, both of which provide unforgettable views and unique geological formations.

Highlights: The Quiraing Circuit takes you through a surreal landscape of pinnacles, cliffs, and plateaus, offering stunning views over the Isle of Skye and the sea. The Old Man of Storr is another iconic hike, leading you to a towering rock formation with panoramic views of the surrounding area.

Tips: Both trails can be busy during peak tourist season, so consider starting early in the day to avoid crowds. The weather on Skye can change rapidly, so come prepared with waterproof gear and sturdy footwear.

6. The Cairngorms: Rothiemurchus and Loch an Eilein

- Distance: 4 miles (6.5 km)
- Duration: 1.5-2 hours
- Difficulty: Easy to moderate
- Starting Point: Rothiemurchus Visitor Centre

The Cairngorms National Park offers a wide range of hiking options, from gentle woodland walks to challenging mountain ascents. One of the most popular and accessible walks in the area is the trail around Loch an Eilein, a picturesque loch surrounded by ancient Caledonian pine forest.

Highlights: The Loch an Eilein trail is perfect for a leisurely walk, with stunning views of the loch and the ruins of a 13th-century castle. The surrounding Rothiemurchus Forest is home to a variety of wildlife, including red squirrels, pine martens, and ospreys.

Tips: This is a family-friendly walk with well-maintained paths, making it suitable for all ages and abilities. If you're looking for a longer hike, several extension options take you deeper into the forest or up into the nearby hills.

7. Ben Nevis: The Highest Mountain in the UK

- Distance: 10.5 miles (17 km)
- Duration: 7-9 hours
- Difficulty: Challenging
- Starting Point: Glen Nevis Visitor Centre

For those seeking a true mountain challenge, Ben Nevis, the highest peak in the UK, is a must-do hike. Standing at 4,413 feet (1,345 meters), the ascent of Ben Nevis is a demanding but rewarding experience, offering stunning views over the surrounding Highlands.

Highlights: The route to the summit follows the well-trodden Mountain Track, also known as the Tourist Route. On a clear day, the views from the top are breathtaking, stretching across the Highlands and, on rare occasions, as far as Northern Ireland.

Tips: The weather on Ben Nevis can be unpredictable, with snow possible even in summer, so proper preparation is essential. Bring plenty of food, water, and layers, and ensure you have a good map and compass as visibility can be poor near the summit.

8. The Pentland Hills: Easy Access to Nature Near Edinburgh

- Distance: Various routes ranging from 2-15 miles
- Duration: 1-5 hours
- Difficulty: Easy to moderate
- Starting Point: Various, including Flotterstone and Hillend

If you're staying in Edinburgh and want to escape to nature, the Pentland Hills are just a short drive or bus ride away. This range of rolling hills offers a variety of walking routes suitable for all levels of fitness, making it a popular spot for both locals and visitors.

Highlights: The Pentland Hills offer stunning views over Edinburgh, the Firth of Forth, and the surrounding countryside. Popular routes include the circular walk from Flotterstone to Scald Law, the highest point in the range, and the gentle stroll around Glencorse Reservoir.

Tips: The Pentlands can be busy on weekends, so consider visiting during the week if you prefer a quieter experience. Many of the paths are well-marked, but it's still a good idea to bring a map and be prepared for changeable weather.

9. The Fife Coastal Path: A Walk Through Scotland's Coastal Heritage

- Distance: 117 miles (188 km)
- Duration: 7-10 days
- Difficulty: Moderate
- Starting Point: Kincardine
- End Point: Newburgh

The Fife Coastal Path takes you on a scenic journey along Scotland's east coast, passing through charming fishing villages, historic sites, and beautiful beaches. This long-distance trail offers a mix of easy walking and more challenging sections, making it accessible to a wide range of walkers.

Highlights: Along the Fife Coastal Path, you'll encounter historic castles, lighthouses, and the famous St. Andrews, the home of golf. The trail also offers stunning views over the North Sea and the chance to spot marine wildlife such as seals and dolphins.

Tips: The trail is well-served by public transport, making it easy to break it into shorter sections if you don't want to tackle the whole route. Be sure to sample some local seafood in the coastal villages along the way.

10. The Borders Abbeys Way: A Walk Through History

- Distance: 68 miles (109 km)
- Duration: 5-7 days
- Difficulty: Moderate
- Starting Point: Jedburgh
- End Point: Circular route

The Borders Abbeys Way takes you on a circular route through the Scottish Borders, passing by the ruins of four medieval abbeys: Jedburgh, Melrose, Dryburgh, and Kelso. This trail offers a unique combination of natural beauty and historical exploration, making it a must-do for history buffs and nature lovers alike.

Highlights: The Borders Abbeys Way offers a journey through Scotland's rich history, with the opportunity to explore the ruins of the abbeys and learn about their significance. The trail also takes you through picturesque countryside, charming towns, and along the River Tweed.

Tips: The Borders Abbeys Way is a relatively gentle trail, but some longer sections require good stamina. Consider taking your time to explore the abbeys and the surrounding areas, as each has its unique charm and history.

Preparing for Your Hike

No matter which trail you choose, preparation is key to a successful and enjoyable hike. Here are some general tips to keep in mind:

Weather: Scotland's weather can be unpredictable, so always check the forecast and be prepared for rain, wind, and sudden temperature changes. Layering is essential, as is having waterproof gear.

Footwear: Invest in a good pair of hiking boots with ankle support, especially if you're tackling more challenging terrain. Make sure your boots are well broken in before starting your hike.

Navigation: While many of Scotland's trails are well-marked, it's always a good idea to carry a map and compass, and know how to use them. GPS devices and trail apps can also be helpful but don't rely solely on technology.

Supplies: Bring plenty of water, snacks, and a packed lunch for longer hikes. It's also a good idea to carry a basic first aid kit and any personal medications you may need.

Respect the Environment: Scotland's landscapes are beautiful but fragile. Follow the Scottish Outdoor Access Code by staying on marked paths, taking your litter home, and leaving wildlife undisturbed.

Wildlife and Nature Reserves

Scotland is a haven for wildlife enthusiasts, offering a rich diversity of species and some of the most beautiful natural habitats in the UK. From the rugged Highlands to the coastal cliffs and tranquil lochs, Scotland's landscapes are home to an array of animals, birds, and marine life. Whether you're an avid birdwatcher, a wildlife photographer, or simply someone who enjoys connecting with nature, Scotland has plenty to offer. This guide will introduce you to Scotland's diverse wildlife and highlight some of the best places to see it, including top birdwatching spots and nature reserves.

Scotland's Diverse Wildlife

Scotland's varied landscapes provide a home for a wide range of wildlife species. Here are some of the key animals and birds you can expect to encounter:

Red Deer: The majestic red deer is Scotland's largest land mammal, commonly found in the Highlands. Autumn is the best time to witness the dramatic rutting season, where stags battle for dominance.

Golden Eagle: One of Scotland's most iconic birds of prey, the golden eagle can be spotted soaring above remote mountains and glens. The Isle of Mull and the Cairngorms are particularly good places to see these magnificent birds.

Scottish Wildcat: Often described as Britain's last remaining wild feline, the elusive Scottish wildcat is a rare and endangered species. It's mainly found in the Highlands, but sightings are extremely rare due to its secretive nature.

Atlantic Puffin: These colourful seabirds are a delight to watch during the breeding season when they nest on Scotland's coastal cliffs and islands. The Isle of May and the Treshnish Isles are popular puffin-spotting locations.

Otters: Scotland's rivers, lochs, and coastal waters are home to otters, which are often seen swimming or playing along the shoreline. The West Coast and the Shetland Islands are particularly good places to spot them.

Red Squirrel: Unlike much of the UK, Scotland still has a healthy population of red squirrels. These charming creatures are often found in the forests of the Highlands, Perthshire, and the Cairngorms.

Seals: Both grey and common seals are abundant around Scotland's coasts, often seen basking on rocks or playing in the water. The Moray Firth and the Orkney Islands are prime spots for seal-watching.

Top Nature Reserves and Birdwatching Spots

Scotland is home to numerous nature reserves and protected areas that offer the perfect environment for wildlife viewing. Here are some of the top spots to visit:

1. Cairngorms National Park: A Highland Wildlife Haven

- Location: Highlands
- Key Species: Red deer, golden eagle, red squirrel, ptarmigan, mountain hare

Cairngorms National Park is the largest national park in the UK and one of the best places in Scotland to experience the country's wildlife. The park's diverse habitats, from ancient Caledonian forests to high mountain plateaus, provide a home for a wide range of species.

Highlights: The Caledonian pine forests of Rothiemurchus and Abernethy are prime spots for spotting red squirrels, pine martens, and capercaillie. The higher elevations are home to species like the ptarmigan and mountain hare, which change their coat colour to white in winter for camouflage in the snow.

Birdwatching: The Cairngorms is also one of the best places in Scotland to see golden eagles, and the RSPB reserve at Loch Garten is famous for its ospreys, which return each year to breed.

2. Isle of Mull: A Wildlife-Rich Island

- Location: Inner Hebrides
- Key Species: Golden eagle, white-tailed eagle, otter, red deer, Atlantic puffin

The Isle of Mull is a must-visit destination for wildlife enthusiasts. The island's diverse landscapes, including rugged coastlines, forests, and moorlands, support a wide variety of species.

Highlights: Mull is one of the best places in Scotland to see both golden eagles and white-tailed eagles, often referred to as "sea eagles." The island's coastal waters are also home to otters, which can be spotted playing along the shoreline, particularly around Loch na Keal.

Birdwatching: During the spring and summer months, the nearby Treshnish Isles are a haven for seabirds, including puffins, razorbills, and guillemots. Boat trips from Mull offer the chance to get up close to these nesting colonies.

3. The Scottish Borders: RSPB Scotland Loch of Strathbeg

- Location: Aberdeenshire
- Key Species: Wintering wildfowl, waders, otters, and occasional rare visitors

This RSPB reserve is one of the best places in Scotland for birdwatching, especially during the winter months when thousands of geese and ducks migrate to the area. Loch of Strathbeg is a vast freshwater loch surrounded by wetlands, offering an ideal habitat for a wide range of species.

Highlights: During the winter, the loch becomes a hub of activity, with large flocks of pink-footed geese, whooper swans, and wigeons. The reserve is also home to otters, which can sometimes be seen along the loch's edges.

Birdwatching: In addition to wintering wildfowl, Loch of Strathbeg is known for attracting rare visitors, such as white-tailed eagles and marsh harriers. The reserve has several hides and viewing points, making it an excellent spot for birdwatchers.

4. The Isle of May: A Seabird Sanctuary

- Location: Firth of Forth
- Key Species: Atlantic puffin, razorbill, guillemot, grey seal

The Isle of May is a small island off the east coast of Scotland that becomes a bustling seabird colony during the breeding season. It's one of the best places in Scotland to see puffins up close, as well as other seabirds.

Highlights: The island's cliffs are teeming with life during the summer months, with puffins, razorbills, and guillemots nesting in large numbers. The surrounding waters are also home to grey seals, which can often be seen basking on the rocks or swimming in the sea.

Birdwatching: Boat trips to the Isle of May run from Anstruther, offering a unique opportunity to experience the island's wildlife. The trips usually include time to explore the island on foot, allowing for close encounters with the seabirds.

5. The Moray Firth: Dolphin Watching Paradise

- Location: Northeast coast
- Key Species: Bottlenose dolphin, grey seal, oystercatcher, gannet

The Moray Firth is one of the best places in Europe to see bottlenose dolphins, which can often be spotted from the shore. The area's coastal waters are rich in marine life, making it a top destination for wildlife enthusiasts.

Highlights: The best place to see dolphins is from Chanonry Point on the Black Isle, where they often come close to shore, especially during the rising tide. The Moray Firth is also home to seals, which can be seen lounging on the rocks or swimming in the sea.

Birdwatching: The coastline of the Moray Firth is a great place to spot seabirds such as oystercatchers, gannets, and terns. The RSPB reserve at Culbin Sands is also worth a visit for birdwatchers, with its mix of dunes, salt marsh, and mudflats attracting a variety of waders and wildfowl.

6. The Flow Country: A Peatland Wilderness

- Location: Caithness and Sutherland
- Key Species: Hen harrier, golden plover, greenshank, red deer

The Flow Country is one of Europe's most important peatland habitats, covering vast areas of Caithness and Sutherland in northern Scotland. This unique landscape of blanket bogs and wetlands is a haven for wildlife, particularly bird species.

Highlights: The Flow Country is home to species that are specially adapted to this wetland environment, including hen harriers, golden plovers, and greenshanks. The area's remote location also makes it one of the best places in Scotland to experience true wilderness.

Birdwatching: The RSPB reserve at Forsinard is a key site for birdwatching in the Flow Country, with its observation tower providing panoramic views of the peatlands. The reserve's walking trails and boardwalks allow visitors to explore this unique habitat and its wildlife.

7. The Orkney Islands: A World of Seabirds and History

- Location: Off the north coast of Scotland
- Key Species: Atlantic puffin, arctic tern, hen harrier, short-eared owl, grey seal

The Orkney Islands offer a rich mix of wildlife and history, with their rugged coastlines and fertile farmland providing a haven for a wide range of species. The islands are particularly known for their seabird colonies, but they also support a variety of other wildlife.

Highlights: The cliffs of Orkney are home to thousands of seabirds, including puffins, arctic terns, and gannets. The islands are also a good place to see hen harriers and short-eared owls, which hunt over the moorland.

Birdwatching: The RSPB reserve at Marwick Head is one of the best places to see seabirds, with its cliffs providing nesting sites for puffins, guillemots, and razorbills. Orkney's wetlands and lochs are also important habitats for waders and wildfowl, making the islands a top birdwatching destination.

Conservation and Responsible Wildlife Viewing

Scotland's wildlife and natural habitats are precious resources that need to be protected. When visiting nature reserves and wildlife sites, it's important to follow guidelines for responsible wildlife viewing. Here are some tips to ensure your visit has minimal impact on the environment:

Keep Your Distance: Avoid disturbing wildlife by keeping a safe distance. Use binoculars or a telephoto lens to observe animals without getting too close.

Stay on Designated Paths: Many nature reserves have designated paths to protect fragile habitats. Stick to these paths to avoid damaging the environment.

Respect Seasonal Restrictions: Some areas may be off-limits during breeding seasons or other sensitive times. Respect any signs or restrictions in place to protect wildlife.

Take Your Litter Home: Always take your litter home with you, and be mindful of leaving no trace behind.

Support Conservation Efforts: Many nature reserves rely on donations and volunteers to continue their conservation work. Consider supporting these efforts by donating or participating in volunteer programs.

Water Activities

Scotland's rugged coastline, tranquil lochs, and flowing rivers make it an ideal destination for water-based activities. Whether you're looking for the thrill of sea kayaking along dramatic cliffs, the serenity of sailing on a quiet loch, or the invigorating experience of wild swimming in pristine waters, Scotland offers a wide range of aquatic adventures. This guide provides an overview of the best water activities in Scotland, including where to go and what to expect.

1. Kayaking and Canoeing: Paddle Through Scotland's Scenic Waters

Kayaking and canoeing are popular activities in Scotland, offering the opportunity to explore the country's stunning landscapes from a unique perspective. From the peaceful inland lochs to the more challenging coastal waters, there's something for every level of paddler.

Sea Kayaking

Best Locations: The west coast of Scotland is renowned for its sea kayaking opportunities, with the Inner Hebrides, Skye, and the Argyll coast being particularly popular. The sheltered waters of Loch Torridon and Loch Hourn also provide excellent sea kayaking experiences.

Highlights: Sea kayaking allows you to explore remote beaches, hidden coves, and dramatic cliffs. You might even encounter wildlife such as seals, dolphins, and seabirds along the way.

Top Experience: The Isle of Skye offers some of the best sea kayaking in Scotland, with its rugged coastline, sea stacks, and crystal-clear waters. The Sound of Arisaig is another fantastic spot, with its sheltered bays and opportunities for wildlife spotting.

Inland Kayaking and Canoeing

Best Locations: Scotland's lochs and rivers provide more tranquil settings for kayaking and canoeing. Loch Lomond, Loch Tay, and Loch Ness are popular choices, offering calm waters and breathtaking scenery. The River Spey and the Great Glen Canoe Trail are also excellent for river paddling.

Highlights: Paddling through Scotland's lochs and rivers allows you to immerse yourself in the country's natural beauty. Glide past ancient castles, lush forests, and rolling hills, with the chance to spot wildlife such as otters, herons, and ospreys.

Top Experience: The Great Glen Canoe Trail is a must-do for adventurous paddlers. This 60-mile route runs from Fort William to Inverness, passing through iconic lochs like Loch Ness and offering a mix of calm waters and more challenging sections.

2. Sailing: Discover Scotland's Maritime Heritage

With its rich maritime history and stunning coastal landscapes, Scotland is a fantastic destination for sailing. Whether you're an experienced sailor or a beginner looking to learn, there are plenty of opportunities to set sail on Scotland's waters.

Sailing in the Inner Hebrides

Best Locations: The Inner Hebrides, including islands like Mull, Islay, and Jura, are prime sailing destinations. The sheltered waters and picturesque anchorages make this area ideal for both day trips and longer voyages.

Highlights: Sailing through the Inner Hebrides offers the chance to explore remote islands, visit historic distilleries, and enjoy the tranquillity of the sea. The region's diverse wildlife, including seals, dolphins, and seabirds, adds to the allure.

Top Experience: The Isle of Mull is a popular base for sailing in the Inner Hebrides. From here, you can explore nearby islands, such as Iona and Staffa, or venture further to the remote Treshnish Isles, known for their puffin colonies.

Sailing on Scotland's Lochs

Best Locations: Scotland's lochs also offer excellent sailing opportunities, with Loch Lomond and Loch Ness being two of the most popular. These inland waters provide a more relaxed sailing experience, with beautiful scenery and plenty of mooring options.

Highlights: Sailing on Scotland's lochs allows you to enjoy the peace and serenity of the water while surrounded by stunning landscapes. Whether you're cruising along the shores of Loch Lomond or exploring the depths of Loch Ness, the experience is unforgettable.

Top Experience: Loch Lomond is a fantastic destination for sailing, with its vast expanse of water and numerous islands to explore. Whether you're hiring a boat or joining a sailing tour, the loch offers a perfect blend of adventure and relaxation.

3. Wild Swimming: Dive into Scotland's Natural Pools

Wild swimming, or open-water swimming, has become increasingly popular in Scotland, with its crystal-clear lochs, rivers, and coastal waters providing some of the best spots for a refreshing dip. Whether you're looking for a secluded spot in the Highlands or a coastal swim on one of Scotland's stunning beaches, wild swimming offers a unique way to connect with nature.

Loch Swimming

Best Locations: Scotland's lochs are perfect for wild swimming, with options ranging from the famous Loch Lomond and Loch Ness to more secluded spots like Loch Morlich in the Cairngorms and Loch Lubnaig in the Trossachs.

Highlights: Loch swimming offers a sense of tranquillity and connection to nature that's hard to match. Whether you're swimming in the shadow of a mountain or floating in the still waters of a remote loch, the experience is both invigorating and calming.

Top Experience: Loch Morlich, located in the Cairngorms National Park, is one of Scotland's most popular wild swimming spots. With its sandy beach and clear waters, it's a great place for a refreshing swim, surrounded by stunning mountain scenery.

Coastal Swimming

Best Locations: Scotland's coastline offers a range of wild swimming opportunities, from the sheltered bays of the west coast to the sandy beaches of the east. The beaches of the Outer Hebrides, such as Luskentyre and Seilebost, are particularly popular for coastal swimming.

Highlights: Coastal swimming in Scotland allows you to experience the raw beauty of the country's seascapes. Whether you're swimming in the turquoise waters of the Hebrides or braving the waves on the East Coast, the experience is exhilarating.

Top Experience: The Isle of Harris is renowned for its stunning beaches and crystal-clear waters, making it a top destination for coastal wild swimming. Luskentyre Beach, with its white sands and turquoise sea, is a favourite among swimmers.

4. Surfing and Windsurfing: Ride the Scottish Waves

Scotland's coastline is not only beautiful but also offers some excellent opportunities for surfing and windsurfing. The country's west coast, in particular, is known for its powerful Atlantic swells, while the east coast offers more sheltered conditions.

Surfing

Best Locations: The west coast of Scotland, especially the Isle of Tiree and the beaches of Thurso, are known for their consistent surf breaks. Other popular spots include Machrihanish on the Kintyre Peninsula and Belhaven Bay near Dunbar.

Highlights: Surfing in Scotland is all about the thrill of riding waves in stunning, often remote, locations. The rugged beauty of the Scottish coastline adds to the excitement, and the lack of crowds means you can often have the waves to yourself.

Top Experience: The Isle of Tiree, known as the "Hawaii of the North," is Scotland's premier surfing destination. With its exposed coastline and consistent swells, Tiree offers excellent surfing conditions for both beginners and experienced surfers.

Windsurfing

Best Locations: Windsurfing is popular on Scotland's lochs and coastal waters, with Loch Insh and Loch Lomond being top spots for inland windsurfing. On the coast, the beaches of the Outer Hebrides and the Moray Firth offer excellent windsurfing conditions.

Highlights: Windsurfing in Scotland allows you to harness the power of the wind while enjoying some of the country's most beautiful landscapes. Whether you're gliding across a loch or catching the wind on the open sea, the experience is exhilarating.

Top Experience: The Moray Firth, with its strong winds and sheltered waters, is a popular destination for windsurfing. The town of Nairn, located on the shores of the firth, is a great base for windsurfing adventures.

5. Scuba Diving: Discover Scotland's Underwater World

Scotland may not be the first place that comes to mind for scuba diving, but its cold waters are home to a surprising array of marine life and underwater attractions. From historic shipwrecks to vibrant coral reefs, Scotland's underwater world is full of surprises.

Wreck Diving

Best Locations: The Orkney Islands, particularly Scapa Flow, are famous for their wreck diving opportunities. This sheltered bay is home to several World War I shipwrecks, making it one of the top wreck diving destinations in the world.

Highlights: Diving in Scapa Flow offers a unique opportunity to explore well-preserved shipwrecks, some of which are over 100 years old. The combination of history and marine life makes it a fascinating dive site.

Top Experience: The wreck of the SMS Markgraf, a German battleship sunk during World War I, is one of the most famous wrecks in Scapa Flow. Diving this wreck is an unforgettable experience, offering a glimpse into Scotland's maritime history.

Reef Diving

Best Locations: Scotland's west coast, particularly around the Isle of Skye and the Inner Hebrides, offers excellent reef diving. The waters around the Isle of Mull and the Sound of Mull are also known for their vibrant marine life.

Highlights: Scotland's reefs are home to a variety of marine species, including colourful corals, sponges, and anemones. You might also encounter seals, lobsters, and even the occasional basking shark.

Top Experience: The waters around the Isle of Skye offer some of the best reef diving in Scotland. The area's clear waters and abundant marine life make for an unforgettable underwater adventure.

Winter Sports

Scotland may not be the first destination that comes to mind for winter sports, but this beautiful country has a surprisingly vibrant winter scene. With its rugged mountains and rolling hills, Scotland offers a range of winter sports activities, from skiing and snowboarding to snowshoeing and ice climbing. The country's winter sports hubs, particularly the Cairngorms and Nevis Range, attract snow enthusiasts from near and far. This section provides an overview of Scotland's winter sports scene, detailing where to go, what to do, and what to expect.

1. Skiing and Snowboarding: Hit the Scottish Slopes

Scotland is home to five main ski resorts, each offering a unique blend of terrain and scenery. While the snow conditions can be unpredictable, when the weather cooperates, Scotland's slopes provide an excellent playground for skiers and snowboarders of all levels.

Cairngorm Mountain Resort

Location: Located near Aviemore in the Cairngorms National Park, Cairngorm Mountain is Scotland's most famous ski resort.

Terrain: With 30 km of skiable terrain, the resort offers a variety of runs, from gentle beginner slopes to challenging black runs. The resort's high altitude (up to 1,230 meters) often provides more reliable snow conditions compared to other Scottish ski areas.

Facilities: Cairngorm Mountain has excellent facilities, including ski and snowboard rentals, a snow school for beginners, and a funicular railway that takes you up to the top of the mountain. The Ptarmigan Top Station offers stunning panoramic views of the surrounding Highlands.

Top Experience: The White Lady run is a must-try for advanced skiers, offering a thrilling descent with fantastic views of the Cairngorms.

Nevis Range Mountain Resort

Location: Situated near Fort William, the Nevis Range is Scotland's highest ski resort, with slopes on the northern side of Aonach Mor.

Terrain: The Nevis Range offers a variety of slopes catering to all skill levels, with a total of 20 km of pistes. The resort is particularly popular with advanced skiers and snowboarders, thanks to its challenging runs and off-piste opportunities.

Facilities: The resort features modern facilities, including a gondola that takes you from the base station to the slopes. There's also a snow park for freestyle enthusiasts and plenty of rental options.

Top Experience: Brave the back corries—an off-piste area known for its steep and deep snow, providing a true adventure for advanced skiers and snowboarders.

Glencoe Mountain Resort

Location: Glencoe Mountain, situated in the west of Scotland, is the country's oldest ski resort and is known for its dramatic scenery.

Terrain: With 20 km of runs and a vertical drop of 808 meters, Glencoe offers a range of slopes for all abilities. The resort is famous for its natural half-pipe and challenging black runs, including the legendary Flypaper, the steepest run in Scotland.

Facilities: Glencoe has a cosy base lodge, equipment rentals, and a ski school. The resort's compact size makes it easy to navigate, and its friendly atmosphere appeals to families and beginners.

Top Experience: The Flypaper is not for the faint-hearted, but if you're an experienced skier looking for a thrill, this steep run is a must.

Glenshee Ski Centre

Location: Glenshee, located in the eastern Highlands, is Scotland's largest ski area, with 36 runs spread across four mountains.

Terrain: Glenshee offers a wide variety of slopes, from gentle greens to challenging blacks. With over 40 km of pistes, there's plenty of room to explore. The Glas Maol area, in particular, is known for its long, sweeping runs.

Facilities: The resort has modern facilities, including numerous lifts, ski and snowboard rentals, and a snow school. The expansive terrain and variety of runs make Glenshee a great choice for all levels of skiers and snowboarders.

Top Experience: The Glas Maol run is one of the longest and most scenic in Scotland, offering stunning views of the surrounding mountains as you carve your way down.

The Lecht Ski Centre

Location: Situated in the eastern Cairngorms, The Lecht is one of Scotland's smaller ski resorts but is perfect for families and beginners.

Terrain: The Lecht offers 20 runs, most of which are beginner and intermediate-friendly. The gentle slopes and well-maintained pistes make it an excellent choice for those new to skiing or snowboarding.

Facilities: The resort has a welcoming atmosphere, with a ski school, rental services, and a café. The Lecht also offers snow tubing and other fun activities for families.

Top Experience: The Buzzard run provides a bit of a challenge for intermediate skiers, with a fun descent and beautiful views of the Cairngorms.

2. Cross-Country Skiing: Explore Scotland's Winter Wilderness

For those who prefer a more peaceful winter experience, cross-country skiing is a fantastic way to explore Scotland's snowy landscapes. The Cairngorms National Park is a prime destination for this activity, offering a network of trails that take you through forests, over hills, and across frozen lochs.

Best Locations

Rothiemurchus Forest: Located near Aviemore, Rothiemurchus Forest is a popular spot for cross-country skiing, with a variety of trails that wind through ancient woodlands and along the shores of Loch an Eilein.

Glenmore Forest Park: Also near Aviemore, Glenmore Forest Park offers well-maintained trails for cross-country skiing. The park's stunning scenery and abundance of wildlife make it a great place to enjoy the winter landscape.

Cairngorm Plateau: For more experienced skiers, the Cairngorm Plateau offers a challenging and rewarding cross-country experience. The high-altitude terrain and deep snow make for an exhilarating adventure.

3. Snowshoeing: A Winter Wonderland on Foot

Snowshoeing is a fantastic way to explore Scotland's winter landscapes at a slower pace. This activity is accessible to all fitness levels and allows you to venture off the beaten path, immersing yourself in the tranquility of the snow-covered wilderness.

Best Locations

Cairngorms National Park: The Cairngorms offer endless opportunities for snowshoeing, with trails that take you through forests, over hills, and up to panoramic viewpoints. The Coire Cas area near Cairngorm Mountain is particularly popular for snowshoeing.

Nevis Range: The Nevis Range is another excellent location for snowshoeing, with routes that offer stunning views of Ben Nevis and the surrounding mountains. The Leanachan Forest, at the base of the range, is a great spot for beginners.

Glencoe: Glencoe's dramatic landscapes are perfect for snowshoeing. The area offers a variety of routes, from gentle valley walks to more challenging mountain ascents.

4. Ice Climbing: Conquer Scotland's Frozen Waterfalls

For those seeking a true adrenaline rush, ice climbing in Scotland is an unforgettable experience. The country's cold winters and rugged terrain create ideal conditions for this challenging sport, with frozen waterfalls and ice-covered cliffs providing a playground for climbers.

Best Locations

Ben Nevis: The north face of Ben Nevis is Scotland's premier ice climbing destination. With routes such as Point Five Gully and The Curtain, Ben Nevis offers some of the most challenging and rewarding ice climbs in the UK.

Cairngorms: The Northern Corries of the Cairngorms also offer excellent ice climbing opportunities. The corries are easily accessible and provide a range of routes, from easier climbs to technical challenges.

Glencoe: Glencoe's dramatic peaks and gullies freeze over in winter, offering a variety of ice-climbing routes. The Aonach Eagach Ridge is a popular spot for those looking to test their skills.

5. Winter Wildlife Watching: Experience Scotland's Cold-Weather Creatures

Winter in Scotland is also a fantastic time for wildlife watching. The snow-covered landscapes provide a stark contrast to the vibrant wildlife that thrives in these conditions.

Best Locations

Cairngorms National Park: The Cairngorms are home to some of Scotland's most iconic winter wildlife, including red deer, mountain hares, and ptarmigans. The RSPB's Abernethy reserve is a great spot to see these animals in their natural habitat.

Isle of Mull: Mull is known for its rich wildlife, and winter is a great time to spot species such as white-tailed eagles and otters. The island's remote landscapes and coastal waters provide a haven for wildlife.

Loch Garten: Located in the Cairngorms, Loch Garten is a fantastic spot for birdwatching, particularly in winter when you might catch sight of the elusive capercaillie.

CHAPTER 7

SCOTLAND'S HISTORY AND HERITAGE

Castles and Historic Sites

Scotland's landscape is dotted with castles and historic sites that tell the tale of a land rich in history, culture, and tradition. From the imposing fortresses that once guarded the Highlands to the elegant palaces that were home to royalty, Scotland's castles and historic sites offer a window into the country's past. Whether you're a history buff or simply captivated by the beauty of these ancient structures, this comprehensive guide will take you on a journey through Scotland's most famous castles and some lesser-known gems.

1. Stirling Castle: The Heart of Scotland's History

Stirling Castle is one of Scotland's most significant historic sites, both for its strategic importance and its role in the country's history. Perched atop Castle Hill, the castle commands views of the surrounding countryside, making it a key military stronghold in centuries past.

History

Strategic Importance: Stirling Castle's location near the River Forth made it a vital stronghold during the Wars of Scottish Independence. It was the site of several key battles, including the Battle of Stirling Bridge in 1297, where William Wallace famously defeated the English army.

Royal Residence: Stirling Castle was also a favoured residence of Scottish kings and queens. It was the childhood home of Mary, Queen of Scots, and played a central role in the lives of many monarchs.

Highlights

The Great Hall: Built by James IV in 1503, the Great Hall is the largest medieval banqueting hall in Scotland. It has been meticulously restored to its original grandeur, with its striking hammer-beam roof and vibrant lime-washed walls.

The Royal Palace: The Renaissance palace within Stirling Castle is a masterpiece of architecture and design. Visitors can explore the opulent apartments of James V and his queen, Mary of Guise, and admire the beautifully crafted Stirling Heads, a collection of carved oak medallions.

The Tapestry Gallery: The castle houses stunning reproductions of the Hunt of the Unicorn tapestries, created in the 16th century. These intricate works of art are a must-see for any visitor.

2. Eilean Donan Castle: Scotland's Iconic Highland Fortress

Eilean Donan Castle is one of Scotland's most photographed and recognizable landmarks. Set on a small island where three sea lochs meet, the castle's stunning location and picturesque appearance make it a favourite for visitors and filmmakers alike.

History

Origins: The original castle on this site was built in the 13th century as a defence against Viking invasions. Over the centuries, it played a key role in the Jacobite uprisings and was destroyed in 1719 during the first Jacobite rebellion.

Restoration: The castle lay in ruins for nearly 200 years before being restored in the early 20th century by Lt. Colonel John MacRae-Gilstrap. The restoration was a labour of love, and today the castle stands as a testament to Scotland's resilience.

Highlights

The Main Keep: Visitors can explore the castle's main keep, which includes a variety of rooms, such as the Banqueting Hall, where the MacRae family history is displayed. The castle's interior is a fascinating blend of medieval and modern influences.

The Views: One of the highlights of Eilean Donan is the view from the castle's battlements. On a clear day, you can see across the lochs to the mountains of Skye and the surrounding Highlands.

Filming Location: Eilean Donan's iconic appearance has made it a popular location for films and TV shows. Fans of the movie Highlander and the James Bond film The World Is Not Enough will recognize the castle from these productions.

3. Dunrobin Castle: A Fairy-Tale Palace in the Highlands

Dunrobin Castle, with its towering spires and fairy-tale architecture, looks like something out of a storybook. Located in the far north of Scotland, this grand castle has been the home of the Earls and Dukes of Sutherland for over 700 years.

History

Origins: The original structure dates back to the early 14th century, but much of what visitors see today is the result of a 19th-century redesign by Sir Charles Barry, the architect behind the Houses of Parliament in London.

Royal Connections: Dunrobin has a rich history connected to Scotland's royal past. It was the site of many significant events, including visits from royalty and its role during the Jacobite risings.

Highlights

The Architecture: Dunrobin Castle's French-inspired design is unique in Scotland. The castle's ornate exterior and manicured gardens are reminiscent of a Loire Valley château.

The Gardens: The castle's gardens, designed in the formal French style, are a major attraction. Visitors can stroll through the perfectly symmetrical parterres and enjoy the stunning views over the Dornoch Firth.

Falconry Displays: One of Dunrobin's most popular attractions is the daily falconry displays. Visitors can watch these majestic birds of prey in action and learn about the ancient art of falconry.

4. Edinburgh Castle: A Fortress of Royal Power

No guide to Scotland's castles would be complete without mentioning Edinburgh Castle, the country's most famous and visited historic site. Perched atop Castle Rock, this iconic fortress dominates the Edinburgh skyline and has played a pivotal role in Scotland's history for centuries.

History

Ancient Origins: The site of Edinburgh Castle has been occupied since at least the Iron Age, and the current castle has stood for more than 900 years. It has been the site of numerous sieges and battles, including during the Wars of Scottish Independence.

Royal Residence: Edinburgh Castle served as a royal residence until the Union of the Crowns in 1603, after which it became more of a military stronghold. It remains one of the most important symbols of Scotland's national identity.

Highlights

The Crown Jewels: The Crown Room houses the Honours of Scotland (the Scottish Crown Jewels), including the Crown, Sceptre, and Sword of State. These precious artefacts are a symbol of Scotland's royal heritage.

The Stone of Destiny: This ancient coronation stone has been used in the crowning of Scottish and English monarchs for centuries. It was returned to Scotland in 1996 and now resides in Edinburgh Castle alongside the Crown Jewels.

St. Margaret's Chapel: This small, 12th-century chapel is the oldest surviving building in Edinburgh. Built by King David I in honour of his mother, Queen Margaret, it is a peaceful retreat within the castle's walls.

5. Urquhart Castle: A Ruin with a View

Urquhart Castle, though now in ruins, is one of Scotland's most evocative historic sites. Located on the shores of Loch Ness, the castle offers spectacular views of the loch and is steeped in history, mystery, and legend.

History

Medieval Stronghold: Urquhart Castle was a major stronghold during the medieval period and played a significant role in the Wars of Scottish Independence. It changed hands several times between the Scots and the English, and its turbulent history is reflected in its ruins.

Jacobite Connection: The castle was partially destroyed in the late 17th century to prevent it from falling into Jacobite hands. Today, its ruins stand as a testament to Scotland's tumultuous past.

Highlights

The Great Tower: The remains of the Great Tower are the most prominent feature of Urquhart Castle. Visitors can climb to the top for panoramic views of Loch Ness and the surrounding Highlands.

Loch Ness: The castle's location on the shores of Loch Ness adds to its allure. Keep an eye out for the famous Loch Ness Monster as you explore the castle grounds!

The Visitor Centre: Urquhart Castle's visitor centre provides a fascinating overview of the castle's history and the legends of Loch Ness. The exhibits include artefacts found on-site and a short film that brings the castle's history to life.

6. Lesser-Known Historic Sites: Hidden Gems of Scotland

While Scotland's famous castles attract the most attention, the country is also home to countless lesser-known historic sites that are equally captivating. These hidden gems offer a more intimate glimpse into Scotland's past and are often less crowded than the major attractions.

Castle Fraser

Location: Located in Aberdeenshire, Castle Fraser is one of Scotland's grandest tower houses. It dates back to the 15th century and is surrounded by beautiful gardens and woodlands.

Highlights: The castle's interior is filled with period furnishings and artwork, and the views from the top of the tower are breathtaking. Don't miss the estate's peaceful nature trails.

Caerlaverock Castle

Location: Caerlaverock Castle, in Dumfries and Galloway, is one of Scotland's most unique castles. Its distinctive triangular shape and moat set it apart from other castles in the country.

Highlights: The castle's history is marked by numerous sieges, and visitors can explore its well-preserved ruins. The surrounding nature reserve is also a haven for wildlife, making it a great spot for a day out.

Duff House

Location: Duff House, in Banff, is a Georgian mansion that served as a royal residence and is now a museum and gallery.

Highlights: The house is filled with fine art, period furniture, and intriguing historical exhibits. The surrounding grounds and gardens are perfect for a stroll.

Museums and Gallerie

Scotland is a country with a rich cultural heritage that spans thousands of years, and nowhere is this more evident than in its museums and galleries. From prehistoric relics to contemporary art, Scotland's museums and galleries offer a deep dive into the nation's history, art, and culture. Whether you're a history enthusiast, an art lover, or simply curious about Scotland's past, these cultural institutions provide a fascinating and enriching experience. This guide will explore some of the top museums and galleries across Scotland, highlighting must-see exhibits and hidden gems.

1. National Museum of Scotland: A Journey Through Time

Located in the heart of Edinburgh, the National Museum of Scotland is one of the country's premier cultural institutions. This museum offers a comprehensive journey through Scottish history, from prehistoric times to the present day, alongside exhibits on global cultures, science, and the natural world.

Key Highlights

The Scottish Galleries: These galleries provide an in-depth look at Scotland's history and identity. Notable exhibits include the Lewis Chessmen, a set of 12th-century chess pieces discovered on the Isle of Lewis, and the Maiden, Scotland's early guillotine. The museum also houses the beautiful Monymusk Reliquary, a piece of early Christian art from the 8th century.

The Natural World: Explore Scotland's wildlife, geology, and natural history in the natural world galleries. The museum's impressive collection includes a full-sized cast of a Tyrannosaurus rex, fossils from Scotland's prehistoric past, and interactive displays that appeal to visitors of all ages.

The Grand Gallery: The museum's central atrium, known as the Grand Gallery, is a striking space filled with larger-than-life objects, including the famous Millennium Clock. The architecture of the gallery itself, with its soaring glass roof and ironwork, is a marvel to behold.

Visitor Tips

Time: Plan to spend at least a few hours exploring the museum's diverse collections. There's so much to see, and it's easy to lose track of time while wandering through the exhibits.

Events and Activities: The museum hosts a variety of temporary exhibitions, events, and family activities throughout the year. Check the museum's calendar before your visit to see what's on.

2. Kelvingrove Art Gallery and Museum: Glasgow's Cultural Gem

Kelvingrove Art Gallery and Museum is one of Glasgow's most beloved cultural institutions, drawing visitors with its eclectic mix of art, history, and natural history exhibits. Housed in a stunning red sandstone building in Kelvingrove Park, this museum offers something for everyone.

Key Highlights

Art Collection: Kelvingrove's art collection is vast and varied, with works spanning centuries and styles. Among the highlights is Salvador Dalí's famous painting Christ of Saint John of the Cross, a powerful and emotive piece that draws art lovers from around the world. The museum also boasts works by the Old Masters, the Glasgow Boys, and Scottish Colourists.

The Armoury and Natural History: One of the most popular exhibits is the arms and armor collection, where visitors can see suits of armor, swords, and weaponry from different periods. The natural history section, featuring taxidermy animals and fossils, is a favourite with younger visitors.

Scottish Art: Kelvingrove's commitment to Scottish art is evident in its collections, which include works by celebrated Scottish artists such as the iconic Charles Rennie Mackintosh. The Mackintosh and Glasgow Style Gallery showcases the life and work of this influential architect and designer.

Visitor Tips

Family-Friendly: Kelvingrove is a fantastic destination for families, with plenty of interactive exhibits and child-friendly displays. The museum is also free to enter, making it an accessible attraction for all.

Events: Like the National Museum, Kelvingrove regularly hosts temporary exhibitions and events, including art workshops and musical performances.

3. The Scottish National Gallery: Masterpieces in the Capital

Located on Edinburgh's Princes Street, the Scottish National Gallery is home to Scotland's national collection of fine art. The gallery's impressive neoclassical building houses works by some of the greatest artists in history, making it a must-visit for art lovers.

Key Highlights

European Masters: The gallery's collection includes masterpieces by European artists such as Titian, Vermeer, Rembrandt, and Botticelli. Among the highlights is Titian's Diana and Callisto, one of the most famous paintings in the collection.

Scottish Art: The Scottish National Gallery is also dedicated to showcasing the best of Scottish art. Visitors can admire works by renowned Scottish painters, including Sir Henry Raeburn's The Reverend Robert Walker Skating on Duddingston Loch, an iconic image of the Scottish Enlightenment.

Impressionism and Post-Impressionism: The gallery's collection also features works by French Impressionists and Post-Impressionists, including pieces by Monet, Degas, and Gauguin.

Visitor Tips

Exhibitions: The Scottish National Gallery frequently hosts special exhibitions that delve deeper into particular artists or themes. It's worth checking what's on during your visit.

Combined Visit: The gallery is close to other major attractions in Edinburgh, such as the Royal Mile and Edinburgh Castle, making it easy to combine a visit to the gallery with a day of exploring the city.

4. The Riverside Museum: Scotland's Museum of Transport and Travel

For those with an interest in transportation and engineering, Glasgow's Riverside Museum is an unmissable destination. Designed by the renowned architect Zaha Hadid, the museum is as impressive for its modern architecture as it is for its fascinating exhibits on transport history.

Key Highlights

Vehicles of All Kinds: The Riverside Museum's vast collection includes everything from vintage cars and motorcycles to locomotives, trams, and bicycles. One of the standout exhibits is the Tall Ship Glenlee, a 19th-century sailing ship moored alongside the museum, which visitors can explore.

Glasgow Street: One of the museum's most popular exhibits is the recreation of a historic Glasgow street, complete with shops, a subway station, and period vehicles. This immersive display offers a glimpse into life in Glasgow during the early 20th century.

Interactive Displays: The museum is packed with interactive exhibits that appeal to visitors of all ages. Whether it's climbing aboard an old tram or experiencing the thrill of a motorcycle race, the Riverside Museum offers a hands-on approach to history.

Visitor Tips

Family Outing: The Riverside Museum is an excellent destination for families, with plenty of activities for children. Admission is free, making it a budget-friendly option.

Photography: Don't forget your camera—the museum's striking design and scenic location along the River Clyde make it a fantastic spot for photography.

5. The Hunterian Museum and Art Gallery: Scotland's Oldest Public Museum

The University of Glasgow is home to the Hunterian, Scotland's oldest public museum. This institution is a treasure trove of art, archaeology, and natural history, with collections that span the globe and millennia.

Key Highlights

The Hunterian Art Gallery: The art gallery's collection includes works by James McNeill Whistler, Charles Rennie Mackintosh, and other notable artists. The gallery also houses the Mackintosh House, a reconstruction of the home of Charles Rennie Mackintosh and his wife, Margaret Macdonald, offering an intimate look at the life and work of this iconic couple.

Roman Scotland: The Hunterian's archaeology collection includes significant finds from Roman Scotland, particularly from the Antonine Wall, a UNESCO World Heritage Site. Visitors can explore Roman artifacts, including sculptures, inscriptions, and everyday items from the ancient frontier.

Natural History and Anatomy: The museum's natural history collection includes everything from fossils and minerals to preserved animals and anatomical specimens. This section of the museum is particularly interesting for those curious about the natural world and the history of science.

Visitor Tips

University Setting: The Hunterian is located within the University of Glasgow, so take some time to explore the beautiful campus and its historic buildings during your visit.

Varied Exhibits: With its diverse collections, the Hunterian offers something for everyone. Plan to spend a few hours here to fully appreciate the breadth of the exhibits.

6. V&A Dundee: Scotland's Design Museum

Opened in 2018, the V&A Dundee is Scotland's first design museum and a bold new addition to the country's cultural landscape. Situated on the Dundee waterfront, the museum is dedicated to showcasing the best of Scottish and international design.

Key Highlights

Scottish Design: The museum's permanent Scottish Design Galleries celebrate Scotland's contribution to the world of design, with exhibits ranging from fashion and textiles to architecture and digital design. Notable items include Charles Rennie Mackintosh's Oak Room and cutting-edge innovations in design technology.

Temporary Exhibitions: The V&A Dundee hosts a range of temporary exhibitions that focus on various aspects of design, from classic fashion houses to futuristic technology. These exhibitions change regularly, so there's always something new to see.

Striking Architecture: Designed by Japanese architect Kengo Kuma, the V&A Dundee is a work of art in itself. The building's unique shape, inspired by Scotland's cliffs, makes it a standout landmark on the Dundee waterfront.

Visitor Tips

Explore Dundee: The V&A Dundee is part of a larger revitalization of the Dundee waterfront. After visiting the museum, take some time to explore the area, including the nearby RRS Discovery, the ship that carried Scott and Shackleton on their Antarctic expedition.

Design Enthusiasts: If you're passionate about design, allow plenty of time to explore the museum's exhibits and enjoy the creative atmosphere.

Clans and Tartans

Scotland's history is deeply entwined with the tales of its clans, the powerful family groups that once dominated the Highlands and beyond. These clans, each with their own distinct identity, traditions, and territories, have left an indelible mark on Scottish culture. Central to this heritage is the tartan, a symbol of clan allegiance and pride. This chapter will delve into the fascinating world of Scotland's clans, exploring their origins, their role in Scottish history, and the enduring significance of tartan in Scottish identity.

1. The Origins of Clans in Scotland

The word "clan" comes from the Gaelic word clann, meaning "children" or "offspring," reflecting the familial nature of these groups. Clans were essentially extended family units, bound together by loyalty to a common ancestor. However, clans were not solely composed of blood relatives; they also included allies and followers who pledged their loyalty to the clan chief.

Clans were particularly prominent in the Highlands, where geography and isolation helped to maintain their distinct identities. Each clan controlled a specific territory, known as a clan lands, and the chief of the clan acted as both leader and protector of his people. In return, the clan members owed their chief allegiance and support, often including military service.

2. The Role of Clans in Scottish History

The clans played a significant role in shaping Scottish history, particularly during the turbulent medieval and early modern periods. Feuds between rival clans were common, with disputes over land, honour, and power often leading to fierce battles. Some of the most famous clan conflicts include the feud between the Campbells and the MacDonalds, which culminated in the infamous Massacre of Glencoe in 1692.

Clans also played a pivotal role in Scotland's struggles against English domination. Many clans supported the Jacobite uprisings of the 17th and 18th centuries, which sought to restore the Stuart monarchy to the British throne. The defeat of the Jacobites at the Battle of Culloden in 1746 marked the beginning of the end for the traditional clan system. In the aftermath, the British government implemented measures to dismantle the power of the clans, including banning the wearing of tartan and the bearing of arms.

3. The Significance of Tartan

Tartan is a patterned cloth consisting of crisscrossed horizontal and vertical bands in multiple colours. While tartan is often associated with kilts and Scottish national dress, its origins are practical rather than symbolic. In the Highlands, tartan was used as everyday clothing, with the distinctive patterns often varying by region rather than by clan.

It wasn't until the 19th century, during the Romantic revival of Scottish culture, that tartan became closely linked with specific clans. The publication of Sir Walter Scott's novels and the visit of King George IV to Scotland in 1822, during which he famously wore a kilt, helped to popularize tartan as a symbol of Scottish identity. Clan chiefs began adopting specific tartans as their official patterns, and the idea of "clan tartans" was born.

Today, tartan is an enduring symbol of Scotland and its clans. Each clan has its own unique tartan, and wearing the tartan of one's clan is a way to express pride in one's heritage. Tartan is also worn on special occasions, such as weddings and Highland games, and remains an integral part of Scottish national dress.

4. Understanding Tartan Patterns and Colours

Each tartan is characterized by its pattern, known as a sett, which consists of a specific arrangement of colours and stripes. Traditionally, the colours used in a tartan were determined by the natural dyes available in the region. Over time, however, tartan patterns have become more standardized, and many modern tartans are registered with the Scottish Register of Tartans.

The meaning behind the colours of tartan can vary. While some believe that certain colours were chosen to represent aspects of the clan's territory or history, others argue that the choice of colours was more practical. For example, the red and green of the Royal Stewart tartan is thought to symbolize the heather and bracken of the Scottish Highlands.

Today, there are thousands of registered tartans, including those associated with clans, regions, and organizations. Some tartans are even created for individuals or special events. Whether you're tracing your ancestry or simply choosing a tartan for a special occasion, there's a wealth of patterns and colours to explore.

5. Famous Scottish Clans and Their Tartans

Scotland is home to many famous clans, each with its own rich history and distinctive tartan. Here are a few of the most well-known:

Clan MacDonald: One of the largest and most powerful clans, the MacDonalds are descended from Somerled, a 12th-century Norse-Gaelic warlord. The MacDonald tartan is a striking pattern of red, green, and black.

Clan Campbell: The Campbells were one of the most influential clans in Scottish history, particularly in the western Highlands. Their tartan, known as Campbell of Argyll, features a simple yet elegant pattern of dark blue and green.

Clan Fraser: Made famous by the Outlander series, the Frasers have a long and storied history. The Fraser tartan is a vibrant mix of red, green, and blue.

Clan MacLeod: Known for their legendary fairy flag, the MacLeods hail from the Isle of Skye. Their tartan, featuring bold yellow and black stripes, is one of the most recognizable.

Clan Stewart: The Stewarts are one of Scotland's royal families, with connections to the Scottish and British thrones. The Royal Stewart tartan, predominantly red with green, blue, and white stripes, is one of the most iconic tartans.

6. Modern-Day Clans and Tartan Culture

While the traditional clan system has largely faded, the sense of clan identity remains strong in Scotland and among the Scottish diaspora. Many people continue to identify with their ancestral clan, and clan gatherings and events are held around the world.

In Scotland, tartan remains an important part of cultural life. Whether it's worn for a wedding, a Highland games competition, or simply as a show of pride, tartan continues to symbolize Scotland's enduring traditions. The annual Edinburgh Tartan Festival and the Royal National Mòd are just two of the many events that celebrate Scotland's rich cultural heritage and its connection to tartan.

In recent years, tartan has also found new life in the fashion world. Designers both in Scotland and internationally have incorporated tartan into their collections, blending tradition with modern style. This has helped to keep tartan relevant in contemporary culture while honouring its historical roots.

7. Tracing Your Clan Heritage

For those interested in tracing their Scottish ancestry, the search for a clan connection can be a rewarding journey. There are numerous resources available, from online databases to local historical societies, that can help you discover your clan roots.

Once you've identified your clan, wearing its tartan is a meaningful way to connect with your heritage. Many people choose to wear their clan's tartan on special occasions, while others incorporate it into their everyday lives. Whether you're wearing a kilt, a scarf, or a tie, your clan's tartan is a tangible link to your Scottish past.

Scottish Legends and Folklore

Scotland's mist-shrouded mountains, ancient castles, and remote lochs provide the perfect backdrop for a rich tradition of myths and legends. These stories, passed down through generations, are deeply ingrained in the country's cultural fabric. From legendary creatures lurking in dark waters to heroic figures who have shaped history, Scotland's folklore offers a fascinating glimpse into the imagination and beliefs of its people. In this chapter, we'll explore some of the most famous myths and legends, including the enigmatic Loch Ness Monster, the legendary tales of Robert the Bruce, and other captivating stories that have left an indelible mark on Scottish identity.

1. The Legend of the Loch Ness Monster

One of Scotland's most enduring and globally recognized legends is that of the Loch Ness Monster, affectionately known as "Nessie." For centuries, tales of a mysterious creature lurking in the depths of Loch Ness, a large freshwater loch in the Scottish Highlands, have captivated imaginations worldwide.

The first recorded sighting of Nessie dates back to the 6th century, when Saint Columba, an Irish monk, reportedly encountered a "water beast" in the River Ness. However, it wasn't until the 20th century that the legend truly took off. In 1933, a photograph surfaced, allegedly showing a long-necked creature swimming in the loch. This image, combined with numerous eyewitness accounts, sparked a global fascination with the Loch Ness Monster.

Despite extensive scientific investigations and sonar explorations, no conclusive evidence of Nessie's existence has been found. Yet, the legend persists, drawing thousands of visitors to Loch Ness each year, all hoping to catch a glimpse of the elusive creature. Nessie has become a symbol of Scotland's mysterious allure, a reminder that some mysteries may never be fully solved.

2. The Heroic Tales of Robert the Bruce

Robert the Bruce, one of Scotland's most celebrated historical figures, is often surrounded by legends that highlight his bravery and determination. The most famous of these tales is the story of Robert the Bruce and the Spider, a story that has inspired generations of Scots.

In 1306, after a series of defeats in his struggle for Scottish independence from England, Robert the Bruce sought refuge in a cave. There, he observed a spider attempting to weave its web. Time and again, the spider failed, but it never gave up. Finally, after many attempts, the spider succeeded. Inspired by the spider's perseverance, Robert the Bruce rallied his forces and eventually won a decisive victory against the English at the Battle of Bannockburn in 1314. This victory secured Scotland's independence, and Robert the Bruce went on to become one of the country's greatest kings.

While the story of the spider may be more legend than fact, it perfectly encapsulates the spirit of resilience and determination that defines Scotland's national character.

3. The Battle of Culloden and the Ghosts of the Highlands

The Battle of Culloden fought in 1746, was the final and most tragic chapter in the Jacobite Rising, a series of attempts to restore the Stuart dynasty to the British throne. The battle, which took place on the windswept moor near Inverness, saw the defeat of the Jacobite forces led by Bonnie Prince Charlie by the British Army.

Culloden is not only remembered for its historical significance but also for the haunting tales that have emerged in its wake. It is said that the battlefield is haunted by the spirits of the fallen Jacobite soldiers, many of whom were brutally slaughtered. Visitors to the site have reported hearing the sounds of battle, the cries of wounded men, and even seeing ghostly apparitions. The eerie atmosphere of Culloden Moor serves as a poignant reminder of the battle's devastating impact on the Highlands and its people.

4. Selkies: The Shape-Shifting Creatures of Scottish Myth

The legends of selkies, shape-shifting creatures that can transform from seals into humans, are among the most enchanting tales in Scottish folklore. These mysterious beings are said to live as seals in the sea but shed their skins to become humans on land.

Selkie legends are particularly prevalent in the Orkney and Shetland Islands, where the sea is a dominant force in daily life. The stories often revolve around selkie women who are captured by humans when their seal skins are stolen. Unable to return to the sea, they are forced to live as humans until they eventually recover their skins and return to the ocean.

Selkie tales are often tinged with sadness and longing, reflecting the deep connection between the people of Scotland and the sea. They also explore themes of freedom, captivity, and the yearning for one's true nature.

5. The Kelpie: Scotland's Water Horse

Another legendary creature that inhabits Scotland's folklore is the kelpie, a shape-shifting water spirit that often takes the form of a horse. Kelpies are said to haunt Scotland's rivers and lochs, luring unsuspecting travellers onto their backs before plunging them into the water to drown.

The most famous kelpie is associated with Loch Ness, where it is believed to have appeared in various forms over the centuries. Some legends suggest that the kelpie can also transform into a human, making it even more dangerous as it can deceive its victims.

The kelpie is often seen as a symbol of the untamed and sometimes treacherous nature of Scotland's waterways. In modern times, the kelpie has been immortalized in the form of the Kelpies, two massive horse-head sculptures located near Falkirk, which pay tribute to Scotland's mythological and industrial heritage.

6. The Legend of the Stone of Destiny

The Stone of Destiny, also known as the Stone of Scone, is a sacred object that has played a central role in Scotland's history and legends. According to tradition, the stone was used in the coronation of Scottish kings for centuries, symbolizing their divine right to rule.

The stone's origins are shrouded in mystery. Some legends claim that it was brought to Scotland from the Holy Land, while others suggest it was used by the biblical figure Jacob as a pillow when he had his famous dream of a ladder reaching to heaven.

In 1296, the stone was seized by King Edward I of England and taken to Westminster Abbey, where it was placed beneath the Coronation Chair, symbolizing English dominance over Scotland. However, in 1950, a group of Scottish students famously stole the stone from Westminster Abbey and returned it to Scotland. Today, the Stone of Destiny resides in Edinburgh Castle, where it continues to be a powerful symbol of Scotland's heritage and identity.

7. The Myth of the Blue Men of the Minch

In the treacherous waters between the Isle of Lewis and the mainland lies the Minch, a sea channel known for its unpredictable currents and strong winds. According to Scottish folklore, the Minch is home to the Blue Men, mythical sea creatures with blue skin who are said to capsize ships and drown sailors.

The Blue Men are described as being human-like in appearance, but with blue skin and the ability to control the weather. They are known for challenging sailors to rhyming contests, and if the sailors fail to complete the rhyme, the Blue Men will drag their ships beneath the waves.

While the Blue Men of the Minch may be little more than a seafarer's tale, they reflect the deep respect and fear that Scotland's coastal communities have for the sea. The legend also highlights the rich oral tradition of storytelling that has preserved these myths for generations.

8. The Fairy Flag of the MacLeods

The Fairy Flag is one of Scotland's most mysterious and treasured artifacts. It belongs to Clan MacLeod, whose ancestral home is Dunvegan Castle on the Isle of Skye. The flag is said to possess magical powers, capable of protecting the clan in times of danger.

According to legend, the flag was a gift from a fairy who fell in love with a MacLeod chieftain. Before returning to the fairy realm, she gave him the flag as a token of her love and a promise that it would protect his descendants. Over the centuries, the flag has been unfurled during battles, and its powers are said to have saved the clan on three occasions.

The Fairy Flag remains one of Scotland's most enigmatic relics, and it continues to be revered by the MacLeod clan and visitors to Dunvegan Castle.

9. The Wulver: Scotland's Benevolent Werewolf

While many cultures fear werewolves as malevolent creatures, Scotland's Wulver is a different kind of beast. Originating from the Shetland Islands, the Wulver is described as a creature with the body of a man and the head of a wolf. Unlike the fearsome werewolves of other legends, the Wulver is considered a benign and solitary creature.

The Wulver is known for its generosity, often seen fishing by a loch and leaving fish on the windowsills of poor families. It is said that the Wulver will not harm humans unless provoked, and it has been known to guide lost travellers to safety.

The legend of the Wulver reflects the close relationship between the people of Scotland and nature, as well as the belief that not all creatures of the wild are to be feared.

National Museum of Scotland

SCAN HERE

HOW TO USE QR CODE

- Open your phone's camera app or download scanner app from play store or apple store
- Point the camera at the QR code for a few seconds (no need to take a photo).
- A link should appear on the display, leading you to the location of the code

Kelvingrove Art Gallery and Museum

in Hall
ctions
displays
archives

Kelvingrove Art Gallery
and Museum car park

Softplay at Kelvinhall

Kelvingrove Art
Gallery and Museum

BrewDog Glasgow
Kelvingrove

Street Food Stop

The Briar Grove Barbers

Elena's Spanish
Bar & Restaurant
Spanish · $$

MacTassos
Greek

SCAN HERE

HOW TO USE QR CODE

- Open your phone's camera app or download scanner app from play store or apple store
- Point the camera at the QR code for a few seconds (no need to take a photo).
- A link should appear on the display, leading you to the location of the code

The Riverside Museum

SCAN HERE

HOW TO USE QR CODE

- Open your phone's camera app or download scanner app from play store or apple store
- Point the camera at the QR code for a few seconds (no need to take a photo).
- A link should appear on the display, leading you to the location of the code

The Hunterian Museum and Art Gallery

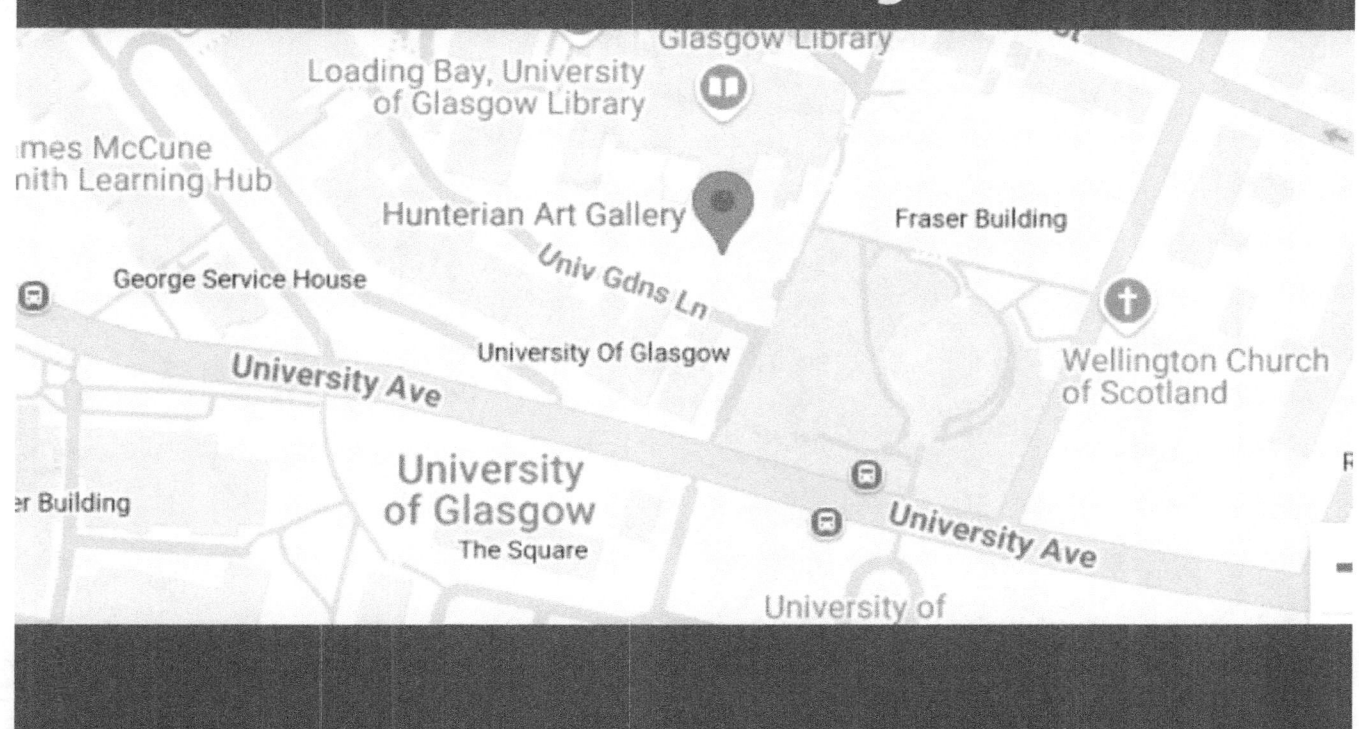

SCAN HERE

HOW TO USE QR CODE

- Open your phone's camera app or download scanner app from play store or apple store
- Point the camera at the QR code for a few seconds (no need to take a photo).
- A link should appear on the display, leading you to the location of the code

V&A Dundee

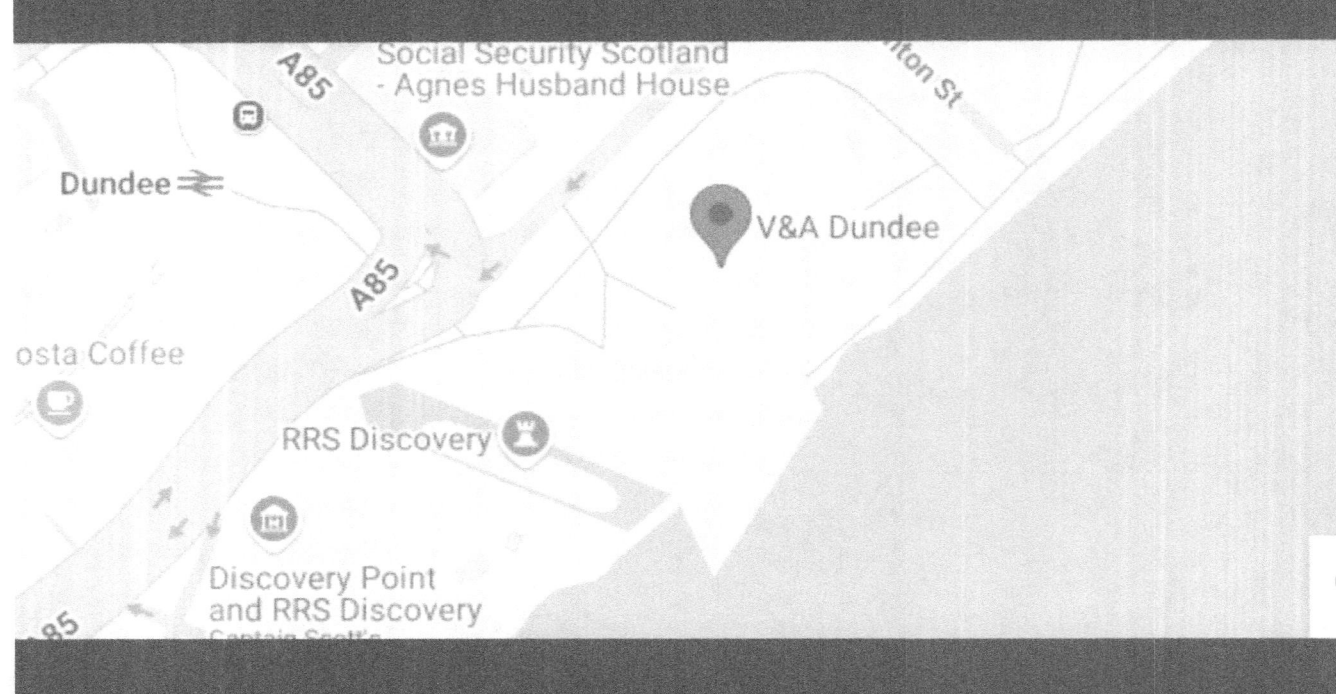

SCAN HERE

HOW TO USE QR CODE

- Open your phone's camera app or download scanner app from play store or apple store
- Point the camera at the QR code for a few seconds (no need to take a photo).
- A link should appear on the display, leading you to the location of the code

V&A Dundee

CHAPTER 8

PRACTICAL INFORMATION

Emergency Contacts and Service

When travelling in Scotland, having access to essential emergency contacts and services is crucial for ensuring your safety and well-being. Whether you're exploring the bustling streets of Edinburgh or hiking in the remote Highlands, knowing who to contact in case of an emergency can provide peace of mind and help you navigate unforeseen situations effectively. In this section, we'll provide a comprehensive list of important phone numbers, including emergency services, embassies, and consulates, along with some practical tips on how to use them.

1. Emergency Services

General Emergency Number – 999 or 112:

In Scotland, as in the rest of the UK, the general emergency number for police, fire, ambulance, and coastguard services is 999 or 112. These numbers are free to call from any phone, including mobiles, and should be used in cases of serious emergencies where immediate assistance is required. When you call, you'll be asked which service you need, and your call will be directed accordingly.

Non-Emergency Police Number – 101:

For non-emergency situations, such as reporting a crime that is not currently happening or seeking advice from the police, you can dial 101. This number connects you to your local police station and is appropriate for issues that do not require an urgent response.

Non-Emergency Medical Advice – NHS 24: 111:

For non-emergency medical advice or if you need to speak with a healthcare professional outside of regular GP hours, you can call NHS 24 by dialing 111. This service provides guidance on health-related concerns and can help you determine whether you need to visit a hospital or seek medical treatment.

2. Embassies and Consulates

If you are a foreign visitor to Scotland, knowing the contact details of your embassy or consulate can be essential in case of legal issues, lost passports, or other situations requiring diplomatic assistance. Below is a list of some key embassies and consulates in Scotland:

United States Embassy in London (Covers Scotland):

- Phone: +44 20 7499 9000
- Emergency Assistance: +44 20 7499 9000 (Ask for the American Citizens Services)
- Website: UK.usembassy.gov
- Canadian Consulate in Edinburgh:
- Phone: +44 131 226 8964
- Emergency Assistance: +44 20 7004 6000 (High Commission in London)
- Website: Canada.ca

Australian Consulate in Edinburgh:

- Phone: +44 131 556 8315
- Emergency Assistance: +44 20 7379 4334 (High Commission in London)
- Website: UK.embassy.gov.au

Irish Consulate General in Edinburgh:

- Phone: +44 131 226 7711
- Emergency Assistance: +44 20 7235 2171 (Embassy in London)
- Website: Dfa.ie

French Consulate General in Edinburgh:

- Phone: +44 131 225 7954
- Emergency Assistance: +44 131 225 7954
- Website: Consulfrance-edimbourg.org

For other nationalities, it's recommended to check with your home country's government website for the most up-to-date contact information for embassies or consulates covering Scotland.

3. Healthcare Services

Hospitals and Clinics:

Scotland has a well-established healthcare system, with numerous hospitals and clinics located throughout the country. In an emergency, you can go directly to the nearest Accident & Emergency (A&E) department, which is open 24 hours a day. Major hospitals like the Royal Infirmary of Edinburgh, Glasgow Royal Infirmary, and Aberdeen Royal Infirmary are equipped to handle a wide range of medical emergencies.

Pharmacies:

Pharmacies, known locally as "chemists," are widely available in Scotland and provide over-the-counter medications, prescription services, and health advice. Many pharmacies have extended hours, and some are open 24 hours, particularly in larger cities. Boots and Lloyds Pharmacy are two of the largest chains in the country.

Dental Emergencies:

If you require urgent dental care while in Scotland, NHS dental services are available. In a dental emergency, contact your regular dentist first. If you're not registered with a dentist, you can call the NHS 24 helpline at 111 for advice on where to go for emergency treatment.

4. Roadside Assistance

If you're driving in Scotland and encounter a vehicle breakdown, several organizations provide roadside assistance. Two of the most popular services are the AA (Automobile Association) and RAC (Royal Automobile Club). Both offer 24/7 roadside recovery services across Scotland.

AA Roadside Assistance:

- Phone: 0800 88 77 66 (Members) or 0800 88 77 88 (Non-members)
- Website: theaa.com

RAC Roadside Assistance:

- Phone: 0333 2000 999 (Members) or 0800 828282 (Non-members)
- Website: rac.co.uk

If you rent a car in Scotland, your rental agreement may include roadside assistance as part of the package. Check with your rental company for details and emergency contact numbers.

5. Lost and Found Services

Police Scotland:

If you lose something valuable while travelling in Scotland, it's advisable to report it to the local police station. Police Scotland operates a nationwide lost property service, where items found in public areas are often turned in. You can contact Police Scotland's non-emergency number, 101, for assistance with lost property.

Public Transport Lost and Found:

If you lose something on public transport, contact the relevant transport provider. For example, ScotRail, Lothian Buses, and the Glasgow Subway each have their own lost and found services. It's a good idea to report the loss as soon as possible, as items are typically kept for a limited time.

6. Travel Insurance

While not a direct emergency contact, having comprehensive travel insurance is highly recommended for any trip to Scotland. Travel insurance can cover unexpected situations such as medical emergencies, trip cancellations, lost luggage, or personal liability. Make sure to carry a copy of your insurance policy, including the emergency contact number for your insurance provider, so that you can quickly access assistance if needed.

Local Laws and Etiquette

When visiting a new country, understanding local laws and cultural norms is essential to ensure a smooth and respectful experience. Scotland, with its rich history and unique cultural identity, has its own set of laws, customs, and etiquette that visitors should be aware of. This section provides an overview of the key legal considerations, as well as tips on how to respect and engage with Scotland's traditions and cultural practices.

1. Legal Considerations

a. Alcohol Consumption and Age Restrictions

In Scotland, the legal drinking age is 18. This means that individuals under the age of 18 are not permitted to purchase or consume alcohol in public places, including pubs, bars, and restaurants. Retailers are required by law to ask for proof of age, so it's advisable to carry identification if you plan on consuming alcohol. Scotland also has strict laws regarding alcohol consumption in certain public areas, particularly in city centres where drinking alcohol on the streets is prohibited.

b. Smoking Regulations

Smoking is banned in all enclosed public spaces in Scotland, including bars, restaurants, and public transportation. This law also extends to certain outdoor areas, such as hospital grounds and school playgrounds. Failure to comply with smoking regulations can result in fines. If you smoke, be sure to look for designated smoking areas, which are usually clearly marked.

c. Driving Laws

Scotland follows the same driving laws as the rest of the UK. Key points to remember include driving on the left side of the road and wearing seat belts at all times. The legal blood alcohol limit for drivers in Scotland is lower than in the rest of the UK, at 50 milligrams of alcohol per 100 millilitres of blood. It is strongly recommended to avoid drinking entirely if you plan on driving. Additionally, using a mobile phone while driving is illegal unless you have a hands-free device. Speed limits are strictly enforced, with urban areas typically having a limit of 30 mph, and motorways usually set at 70 mph.

d. Drug Laws

Scotland has strict drug laws and the possession, use, or distribution of illegal substances is a criminal offence with severe penalties. Visitors should be aware that even small amounts of controlled substances can lead to arrest and prosecution. It's important to respect these laws and avoid any involvement with illegal drugs during your stay.

e. Respecting Privacy

Scots value their privacy, and it is important to be mindful of this, especially when taking photographs or engaging in conversations with locals. Always ask for permission before photographing individuals or private property, particularly in more rural or traditional communities where privacy is highly regarded.

2. Cultural Etiquette

a. Greetings and Social Interactions

Scots are generally warm and friendly people, but they also value politeness and respect. A firm handshake is the most common form of greeting, particularly in formal settings. When addressing someone, it's customary to use their title and last name until invited to do otherwise. While Scots are often open to conversation, it's important to respect personal space and not to be overly familiar with strangers.

b. Tipping Culture

Tipping is appreciated but not mandatory in Scotland. In restaurants, it's common to leave a tip of around 10-15% if the service has been good. Some restaurants may include a service charge in the bill, so it's worth checking before leaving an additional tip. Tipping is also customary for taxi drivers, hotel staff, and tour guides, though smaller amounts are generally expected.

c. Respecting Traditions

Scotland has a deep-rooted cultural heritage, and traditions such as Highland games, Burns Night, and the celebration of St. Andrew's Day are significant events. When participating in or observing these traditions, it's important to show respect for the customs and practices involved. For example, during Burns Night, the recitation of Robert Burns' poetry is a cherished tradition, and participating in the toasts and festivities with enthusiasm is encouraged.

d. Language Considerations

While English is the primary language spoken in Scotland, you may also encounter Gaelic, particularly in the Highlands and Islands. While it's not necessary to speak Gaelic, showing an interest in the language or attempting to learn a few basic phrases can be appreciated by locals. Scots also have a distinct dialect that may include words and expressions unfamiliar to visitors, so don't hesitate to ask for clarification if you're unsure of something.

e. Dress Code

Scotland's dress code is generally relaxed, especially in rural areas. However, if you're attending a formal event or visiting certain establishments, such as upscale restaurants or clubs, dressing smartly is expected. Traditional Scottish dress, such as kilts, is worn for special occasions, and if you're invited to such an event, you may be encouraged to wear traditional attire. If you choose to do so, it's important to wear it correctly and with respect for the cultural significance it holds.

3. Social Norms and Unwritten Rules

a. Queuing

Queuing, or lining up, is an important part of Scottish social etiquette. Whether waiting for a bus, at a supermarket checkout, or in a bank, it's expected that you'll wait your turn in line. Pushing ahead or cutting the queue is considered extremely rude and is likely to provoke a negative response.

b. Punctuality

Punctuality is valued in Scotland, particularly in professional and formal settings. If you have an appointment or a reservation, arriving on time is important. Being late without a good reason can be seen as disrespectful. If you are running late, it's polite to inform the person you're meeting as soon as possible.

c. Environmental Awareness

Scots are generally very environmentally conscious, and this is reflected in the country's strong focus on recycling and reducing waste. When travelling in Scotland, it's important to dispose of rubbish correctly, using recycling bins where available. Littering is not only frowned upon but can also result in fines. When exploring natural areas, following the "Leave No Trace" principles is crucial to preserving Scotland's beautiful landscapes.

d. Religion and Beliefs

Scotland is a country with diverse religious beliefs, including Christianity, Islam, Judaism, and others. While Scotland is generally a secular society, religion remains an important aspect of life for many people. When visiting places of worship or attending religious events, dressing modestly and behaving respectfully is important. It's also worth noting that Sundays can be quieter in some areas, with reduced public transport and shop hours, reflecting traditional Christian practices.

Accessibility Information

Scotland is a country of stunning landscapes, rich history, and vibrant culture, and it strives to be accessible to all visitors, including those with disabilities. Travelling with accessibility needs can present unique challenges, but Scotland has made significant strides in ensuring that its attractions, accommodations, and transportation are as inclusive as possible. This section provides a comprehensive guide to accessible travel in Scotland, offering valuable resources and tips for travellers with disabilities.

1. Accessible Accommodations

a. Hotels and Guesthouses

Many hotels and guesthouses in Scotland have made efforts to provide accessible accommodations for travellers with disabilities. In cities like Edinburgh, Glasgow, and Inverness, you'll find a range of options, from luxury hotels to budget-friendly guesthouses, that offer accessible rooms. These rooms typically feature wider doorways, roll-in showers, grab bars, lowered beds, and other amenities designed to accommodate various needs.

When booking your accommodation, it's important to communicate your specific requirements in advance to ensure that your needs are met. Many booking platforms, such as Booking.com and Airbnb, allow you to filter search results to find properties with accessibility features. Additionally, organizations like Euan's Guide provide reviews and information on accessible places to stay, dine, and visit in Scotland.

b. Self-Catering and Holiday Rentals

For those seeking more independence, self-catering cottages and holiday rentals can also be a great option. Some properties are specifically designed with accessibility in mind, offering step-free access, adapted kitchens and bathrooms, and ground-floor bedrooms. The National Accessible Scheme (NAS) rates accommodations based on their level of accessibility, helping you to choose the right option for your needs.

c. Camping and Glamping

Accessible camping and glamping sites are increasingly available across Scotland. These sites often offer accessible facilities, including level pitches, accessible toilets, and showers. Glamping, which combines camping with comfort, often provides options such as cabins or yurts with step-free access and adapted interiors. It's advisable to contact the campsite directly to discuss your specific needs before booking.

2. Transportation and Getting Around

a. Public Transportation

Scotland's public transportation system is generally accessible, with ongoing improvements to ensure inclusivity. Buses in major cities like Edinburgh and Glasgow are equipped with low floors, ramps, and designated spaces for wheelchair users. Drivers are trained to assist passengers with disabilities, and priority seating is available for those with mobility needs.

Scotland's train network is also making strides in accessibility. Many train stations offer step-free access, elevators, and accessible toilets. Onboard, most trains have designated spaces for wheelchairs and accessible toilets. If you require assistance boarding or alighting a train, you can arrange this through the Passenger Assist service, which is available across the UK rail network.

b. Taxis and Ride-Sharing

Accessible taxis, also known as wheelchair-accessible vehicles (WAVs), are available in most Scottish cities and larger towns. These taxis are equipped with ramps or lifts and can accommodate both manual and powered wheelchairs. It's recommended to book in advance, especially during busy periods. Ride-sharing services like Uber also offer accessible options in some areas, though availability may be limited outside major cities.

c. Car Rentals

If you prefer the freedom of driving, several car rental companies in Scotland offer vehicles adapted for drivers with disabilities. These vehicles may include hand controls, left-foot accelerators, and swivel seats. It's important to arrange this in advance, as adapted vehicles may not be readily available at all rental locations. Additionally, blue badge holders (disabled parking permits) can benefit from designated parking spaces in cities, towns, and tourist attractions across Scotland.

d. Air Travel and Airports

Scotland's major airports, including Edinburgh, Glasgow, and Aberdeen, are equipped with facilities to assist travellers with disabilities. These airports offer step-free access, accessible restrooms, and designated seating areas. Special assistance, such as help with boarding and disembarking, can be arranged through your airline or directly with the airport's assistance services. It's advisable to notify your airline of any specific needs at least 48 hours before your flight.

3. Accessible Attractions and Activities

a. Historic Sites and Museums

Scotland is home to many historic sites, castles, and museums, many of which have made efforts to improve accessibility. For example, Edinburgh Castle offers wheelchair access to certain areas, as well as a courtesy vehicle for those with mobility challenges. The National Museum of Scotland in Edinburgh provides wheelchair access throughout the building, along with accessible toilets and hearing loops for visitors with hearing impairments.

Similarly, the Kelvingrove Art Gallery and Museum in Glasgow and the Riverside Museum offer step-free access, lifts, and accessible facilities. Many attractions provide detailed accessibility information on their websites, so it's worth checking ahead of your visit.

b. Outdoor Activities and Nature Trails

Scotland's natural beauty is a significant draw for visitors, and efforts have been made to make the great outdoors more accessible. The Loch Lomond & The Trossachs National Park, for instance, offers accessible trails, viewing platforms, and facilities. Some of the park's trails are designed specifically for wheelchair users and those with limited mobility, providing opportunities to enjoy Scotland's stunning landscapes.

For wildlife enthusiasts, the Royal Society for the Protection of Birds (RSPB) reserves, such as Loch Leven and Insh Marshes, offer accessible hides and pathways, making birdwatching and nature walks more inclusive. Additionally, organizations like Disabled Ramblers Scotland organize group outings and provide information on accessible routes.

c. Festivals and Events

Scotland hosts a wide array of festivals and events throughout the year, and many are committed to ensuring accessibility for all attendees. The Edinburgh Festival Fringe, for example, provides accessible venues, performances with British Sign Language (BSL) interpretation, and assistance for visitors with mobility needs. It's advisable to contact the event organizers in advance to discuss your specific requirements and to ensure a seamless experience.

4. Resources and Support Services

a. Euan's Guide

Euan's Guide is a valuable resource for travellers with disabilities, offering reviews and information on accessible places across Scotland. The website features user-generated reviews of hotels, restaurants, attractions, and more, allowing you to plan your trip with confidence. The guide also provides tips and advice from fellow travellers with disabilities, helping you navigate the challenges of accessible travel.

b. VisitScotland's Accessible Tourism Program

VisitScotland, the national tourism organization, has an Accessible Tourism Program aimed at improving and promoting accessibility in Scotland's tourism industry. Their website offers a wealth of information on accessible attractions, accommodations, and transportation, as well as resources to help businesses enhance their accessibility.

c. Local Disability Organizations

Several local organizations in Scotland offer support and resources for travellers with disabilities. For example, Capability Scotland provides information on accessible services and facilities, while Disability

Information Scotland offers advice on a wide range of accessibility-related topics. These organizations can be invaluable in helping you plan your trip and ensuring that your needs are met.

5. Tips for Accessible Travel in Scotland

a. Plan Ahead

One of the most important tips for accessible travel is to plan ahead. Research accommodations, transportation options, and attractions to ensure they meet your specific needs. Contact service providers directly to confirm accessibility features and to arrange any necessary assistance.

b. Pack Accordingly

When packing for your trip, consider any mobility aids or equipment you may need. If you require specific medical supplies, ensure you have enough for the duration of your stay, as well as any necessary documentation for carrying medication or equipment through customs.

c. Be Prepared for Weather

Scotland's weather can be unpredictable, so it's important to be prepared. Bring appropriate clothing and accessories, such as waterproof jackets, sturdy footwear, and any items that will help you stay comfortable in varying conditions.

d. Use Technology to Your Advantage

Technology can be a great ally in accessible travel. Use apps and websites to find accessible routes, attractions, and services. Google Maps, for example, offers information on wheelchair-accessible routes in some areas, and apps like AccessAble provide detailed accessibility information for venues across Scotland.

Travel Apps and Resources

In today's digital age, planning and navigating your travels has never been easier, thanks to the abundance of apps, websites, and guidebooks available at your fingertips. Scotland, with its rich history, vibrant culture, and stunning landscapes, can be fully appreciated with the right resources to help you along the way. Whether you're looking to book accommodations, find the best restaurants, explore off-the-beaten-path destinations, or simply stay organized, this guide provides you with a comprehensive list of the most useful travel apps, websites, and guidebooks to complement your Scottish adventure.

1. Essential Travel Apps for Scotland

a. Google Maps

A staple for travellers worldwide, Google Maps is indispensable when navigating Scotland's cities, towns, and countryside. The app provides detailed maps, real-time traffic updates, and public transportation options. Use it to find walking directions through Edinburgh's historic streets, driving routes through the Highlands, or to locate nearby restaurants, shops, and attractions. The offline maps feature is particularly useful when exploring remote areas with limited internet access.

b. VisitScotland App

The official tourism app from VisitScotland is an excellent companion for your trip. It offers a wealth of information on attractions, events, accommodations, and activities across the country. The app allows you to create personalized itineraries, discover hidden gems, and access insider tips from locals. It's a one-stop resource for everything you need to know about travelling in Scotland.

c. Rome2rio

If you're looking to explore multiple destinations within Scotland, Rome2rio is a fantastic tool for planning your routes. The app provides various transportation options, including flights, trains, buses, ferries, and driving routes, along with estimated travel times and costs. Whether you're travelling from Glasgow to the Isle of Skye or planning a day trip to Stirling, Rome2rio helps you find the most convenient and efficient ways to get there.

d. ScotRail App

For those planning to travel by train, the ScotRail app is essential. It provides real-time train schedules, ticket booking options, and platform information. The app also offers service updates and allows you to purchase tickets directly from your phone, making your journey smoother and more efficient. Scotland's rail network connects major cities, scenic routes, and remote destinations, making it a great way to explore the country.

e. Citymapper

Citymapper is a highly useful app for navigating urban areas, particularly in larger cities like Edinburgh and Glasgow. It offers real-time public transportation information, including buses, trams, trains, and even bike-sharing options. The app provides step-by-step directions, estimated travel times, and alerts for service disruptions. It's especially handy for first-time visitors trying to make sense of a new city's transit system.

f. Airbnb

If you're looking for unique accommodations, Airbnb offers a wide range of options, from cosy cottages in the countryside to stylish apartments in the heart of Edinburgh. The app allows you to filter search results by accessibility, amenities, and location, making it easier to find the perfect place to stay. Additionally, Airbnb's Experiences feature offers locally-led tours and activities that provide an authentic taste of Scottish culture.

g. XE Currency

Travelling from abroad? The XE Currency app is a must-have for converting currencies on the go. It provides up-to-date exchange rates and allows you to convert prices in real time, helping you manage your budget and avoid any surprises. Whether you're shopping for souvenirs in a Glasgow market or dining out in Inverness, this app ensures you know exactly how much you're spending.

h. TripIt

TripIt is a powerful travel organizer that helps you keep all your travel plans in one place. After booking your flights, accommodations, and activities, simply forward your confirmation emails to TripIt, and the app will create a detailed itinerary for you. It's a great way to stay organized, especially if you have multiple bookings and activities planned during your stay in Scotland.

i. Weather Apps

Given Scotland's unpredictable weather, having a reliable weather app is crucial. Apps like Met Office Weather or AccuWeather provide detailed forecasts, including hourly updates, weather warnings, and real-time radar maps. These apps can help you plan your daily activities and pack appropriately for the ever-changing Scottish climate.

2. Essential Websites for Scottish Travel

a. VisitScotland (visitscotland.com)

The VisitScotland website is the official tourism portal for Scotland, offering comprehensive information on everything from accommodations and attractions to events and travel tips. It's an invaluable resource for planning your trip, with detailed guides on Scotland's regions, history, culture, and outdoor activities. The site also features user reviews, travel itineraries, and special offers, making it a go-to resource for all things Scotland.

b. National Trust for Scotland (nts.org.uk)

If you're interested in Scotland's historic sites, gardens, and nature reserves, the National Trust for Scotland website is a must-visit. The site provides information on hundreds of properties under the Trust's care, including castles, battlefields, and scenic landscapes. You can explore visitor guides, check opening times, and purchase tickets online. The website also offers membership options, which include free entry to many sites.

c. Walkhighlands (walkhighlands.co.uk)

For outdoor enthusiasts, Walkhighlands is an essential resource. The website offers detailed guides to hiking trails across Scotland, ranging from easy walks to challenging mountain climbs. Each route includes maps, descriptions, and user reviews, as well as information on nearby accommodations and facilities. Whether you're exploring the Highlands, the Cairngorms, or the Isle of Skye, Walkhighlands is your go-to guide for planning an unforgettable outdoor adventure.

d. Historic Environment Scotland (historic environment.scot)

Historic Environment Scotland is the body responsible for preserving Scotland's historic sites and monuments. Their website provides extensive information on castles, abbeys, and archaeological sites across the country. You can find details on opening hours, ticket prices, and guided tours, as well as educational resources and interactive maps. The site is particularly useful for history buffs looking to delve deeper into Scotland's rich heritage.

e. ScotRail (scotrail.co.uk)

For train travel information, the official ScotRail website is an excellent resource. It offers train schedules, route maps, and ticket booking options, as well as details on special scenic routes like the West Highland Line and the Borders Railway. The website also provides travel advice, accessibility information, and service updates, ensuring you have everything you need for a smooth rail journey.

f. Undiscovered Scotland (undiscoveredscotland.co.uk)

Undiscovered Scotland is an independent guide that offers in-depth information on Scotland's lesser-known destinations. The website features detailed descriptions of towns, villages, and attractions off the beaten path, as well as practical travel advice. It's a great resource for those looking to explore Scotland beyond the usual tourist spots and discover hidden gems across the country.

g. Edinburgh Festivals (edinburghfestivalcity.com)

If you're visiting Scotland during the summer festival season, the Edinburgh Festivals website is an essential tool. It provides information on all major festivals in the city, including the Edinburgh International Festival, the Edinburgh Festival Fringe, and the Edinburgh International Book Festival. You can browse event listings, purchase tickets, and find out about accessibility options, ensuring you make the most of your festival experience.

3. Tips for Using Travel Apps and Resources

a. Stay Connected

To make the most of travel apps and websites, it's important to stay connected while on the go. Consider purchasing a local SIM card or an international data plan to ensure you have internet access throughout your trip. Many public places, including cafes, hotels, and tourist attractions, offer free Wi-Fi, but having your connection will give you the flexibility to access information anytime, anywhere.

b. Download Offline Content

When exploring remote areas or regions with spotty internet coverage, downloading maps, guides, and travel documents for offline use is a smart move. Google Maps and several guidebook apps offer offline functionality, ensuring you have access to essential information even when you're off the grid.

c. Keep Your Devices Charged

With heavy use of apps and navigation tools, your devices' batteries may drain faster than usual. Carry a portable charger or power bank to keep your phone and other gadgets charged throughout the day. This is particularly important when hiking, driving long distances, or spending extended time outdoors.

d. Cross-Reference Information

While travel apps and websites are incredibly useful, it's always a good idea to cross-reference information with multiple sources. Check reviews, compare itineraries, and consult guidebooks to ensure you're getting the most accurate and up-to-date advice. This approach will help you avoid potential pitfalls and make well-informed decisions during your trip.

CHAPTER 9

ITINERARY

Suggested Itineraries: Tailored Adventures for Every Traveller

Planning a trip to Scotland can be both exciting and overwhelming, given the sheer diversity of attractions, landscapes, and experiences on offer. To help you make the most of your time, this section presents a variety of suggested itineraries, each tailored to different interests and travel styles. Whether you're a culture enthusiast, a nature lover, or travelling with family, these itineraries are designed to guide you through Scotland's most iconic and lesser-known destinations, ensuring a memorable journey.

1. The Classic Scotland Tour: A Week-Long Cultural Exploration

Day 1: Arrival in Edinburgh

Begin your journey in Scotland's historic capital, Edinburgh. Spend the day exploring the Royal Mile, visiting Edinburgh Castle, and wandering through the medieval streets of the Old Town. In the evening, enjoy traditional Scottish cuisine at a local restaurant.

Day 2: Edinburgh's Cultural Gems

Dedicate the second day to Edinburgh's rich cultural offerings. Visit the National Museum of Scotland, take a walk up Arthur's Seat for panoramic views, and explore the Georgian architecture of the New Town. Consider attending an evening performance at the Edinburgh Playhouse or a local music venue.

Day 3: Stirling and Loch Lomond

Travel to Stirling to visit the iconic Stirling Castle and the Wallace Monument. In the afternoon, head to Loch Lomond and The Trossachs National Park. Enjoy a boat tour on Loch Lomond or take a scenic hike. Stay overnight in a charming village-like Luss.

Day 4: Glasgow's Art and Architecture

Drive to Glasgow, Scotland's largest city, known for its vibrant arts scene. Explore the Kelvingrove Art Gallery, the Riverside Museum, and the architectural wonders of Charles Rennie Mackintosh. Spend the evening experiencing Glasgow's lively nightlife or dining in the trendy West End.

Day 5: The Highlands and Inverness

Head north to the Highlands, stopping at Loch Ness en route to Inverness. Visit Urquhart Castle and keep an eye out for the elusive Loch Ness Monster. Spend the night in Inverness, the gateway to the Highlands.

Day 6: Isle of Skye Adventure

Take a day trip to the Isle of Skye, known for its rugged landscapes and dramatic scenery. Explore the Old Man of Storr, the Quiraing, and the Fairy Pools. Return to Inverness in the evening or stay overnight on Skye.

Day 7: Return to Edinburgh via Pitlochry

On your way back to Edinburgh, stop in the picturesque town of Pitlochry, known for its Victorian architecture and scenic setting. Visit a whisky distillery or take a walk in the surrounding hills. Arrive in Edinburgh in the evening, concluding your cultural tour of Scotland.

2. Scotland's Natural Wonders: A Nature-Focused Adventure

Day 1: Arrival in Glasgow and Loch Lomond

Begin your nature-focused adventure in Glasgow, then head straight to Loch Lomond and The Trossachs National Park. Spend the day exploring the park's lakes, forests, and mountains. Consider a hike up Ben Lomond or a boat tour on the loch.

Day 2: Glencoe and the West Highland Way

Travel to Glencoe, one of Scotland's most dramatic landscapes. Take a hike along the West Highland Way, or explore the Glencoe Visitor Centre to learn about the area's history and geology. Stay overnight in Fort William, at the foot of Ben Nevis.

Day 3: Ben Nevis and the Great Glen

Challenge yourself with a hike up Ben Nevis, the UK's highest peak, or opt for a more leisurely exploration of the Great Glen. Visit the Caledonian Canal or take a scenic drive along the Great Glen Way, passing through Loch Ness and Fort Augustus.

Day 4: Isle of Mull and Iona

Take a ferry to the Isle of Mull, known for its rugged coastline and abundant wildlife. Visit the town of Tobermory, with its colourful waterfront, and consider a side trip to the nearby Isle of Iona, a historic and spiritual site. Stay overnight on Mull.

Day 5: Cairngorms National Park

Head east to Cairngorms National Park, a vast wilderness area offering opportunities for hiking, wildlife watching, and adventure sports. Visit the Highland Wildlife Park or take the Cairngorm Mountain Railway for stunning views. Stay overnight in Aviemore or a nearby village.

Day 6: The Northeast Coast and Dunnottar Castle

Travel to the northeast coast, where you'll find rugged cliffs, sandy beaches, and the dramatic ruins of Dunnottar Castle. Spend the day exploring the coastline and nearby towns like Stonehaven or Aberdeen. Stay overnight in Aberdeen or Inverness.

Day 7: Return to Edinburgh via the East Neuk

On your return to Edinburgh, take the coastal route through the East Neuk of Fife, known for its charming fishing villages. Stop in St. Andrews to visit the famous golf course and the historic university. Arrive in Edinburgh in the evening, completing your nature-filled journey.

3. Family-Friendly Scotland: Fun for All Ages

Day 1: Arrival in Edinburgh

Kick off your family adventure in Edinburgh, by exploring the city's family-friendly attractions. Visit Edinburgh Zoo, where you can see giant pandas, or take a tour of the Camera Obscura and World of Illusions. In the evening, enjoy a relaxed dinner at a family-friendly restaurant.

Day 2: Edinburgh's Castles and Museums

Spend the day visiting Edinburgh Castle, where kids can learn about Scotland's history through interactive exhibits. Next, head to the National Museum of Scotland, which offers a wide range of exhibits that appeal to all ages. Consider a visit to the Royal Botanic Garden for a peaceful afternoon stroll.

Day 3: Stirling and Blair Drummond Safari Park

Travel to Stirling to explore Stirling Castle, which offers activities and exhibits tailored for children. In the afternoon, visit Blair Drummond Safari Park, where the whole family can enjoy animal encounters, rides, and play areas. Stay overnight in Stirling or Glasgow.

Day 4: Loch Lomond and The Trossachs

Head to Loch Lomond for a day of outdoor fun. Take a family-friendly hike, rent bikes, or enjoy a boat ride on the loch. Visit the Loch Lomond SEA LIFE Aquarium, where kids can learn about marine life. Stay overnight in a family-friendly accommodation near the park.

Day 5: Glasgow's Science and Adventure

Spend the day in Glasgow, starting with a visit to the Glasgow Science Centre, where kids can engage with hands-on exhibits and interactive displays. In the afternoon, explore the Riverside Museum, which focuses on transportation history. Consider an evening at a family-friendly show or event in the city.

Day 6: Highland Wildlife Park and Aviemore

Travel to the Highlands and visit the Highland Wildlife Park, where you can see native and exotic animals in a natural setting. Spend the afternoon in Aviemore, where you can enjoy activities like swimming, biking, or a visit to the Landmark Forest Adventure Park. Stay overnight in Aviemore.

Day 7: The Isle of Skye or Loch Ness

For your final day, choose between a trip to the Isle of Skye, with its fairy-tale landscapes and family-friendly hikes, or a visit to Loch Ness, where kids can search for the legendary Nessie. Explore the area, take a boat tour, and enjoy a picnic before returning to your base.

4. Scotland for History Buffs: A Journey Through Time

Day 1: Arrival in Edinburgh and the Royal Mile

Start your historical journey in Edinburgh, where you'll explore the Royal Mile's rich history. Visit Edinburgh Castle, St Giles' Cathedral, and the Palace of Holyroodhouse. In the evening, take a ghost tour to learn about the city's darker past.

Day 2: Stirling and Bannockburn

Travel to Stirling to visit the site of the Battle of Bannockburn and the Wallace Monument, dedicated to Scotland's national hero, William Wallace. Spend the afternoon at Stirling Castle, learning about its role in Scotland's history. Stay overnight in Stirling or Perth.

Day 3: Perthshire's Castles and Scone Palace

Explore Perthshire, starting with a visit to Scone Palace, the crowning place of Scottish kings. Continue to visit Blair Castle, known for its unique history and beautiful grounds. End the day in Pitlochry, with an optional visit to the nearby Edradour Distillery.

Day 4: The Highlands and Culloden Battlefield

Head to the Highlands to visit Culloden Battlefield, the site of the last battle on British soil. Explore the visitor centre and walk the battlefield, reflecting on this pivotal moment in Scottish history. Stay overnight in Inverness or the surrounding area.

Day 5: The Isle of Skye's Historic Sites

Take a day trip to the Isle of Skye, focusing on its historical sites. Visit Dunvegan Castle, the oldest continuously inhabited castle in Scotland,

and explore the island's ancient stone structures, such as the Brochs and the Neolithic gravesites. Return to Inverness or stay overnight on Skye.

Day 6: The Northeast Coast and Elgin Cathedral

Travel to the northeast coast to visit Elgin Cathedral, one of Scotland's most beautiful medieval ruins. Continue to explore other historical sites in the area, such as Spynie Palace and Duffus Castle. Stay overnight in Aberdeen or the surrounding area.

Day 7: Return to Edinburgh via St. Andrews

On your return to Edinburgh, stop in St. Andrews, the birthplace of golf and home to Scotland's oldest university. Visit St. Andrews Cathedral and Castle, then enjoy a leisurely walk along the coastal path before heading back to Edinburgh, completing your historical journey.

Day Trips and Excursions: Exploring Beyond the Cities

While Scotland's cities offer a wealth of experiences, the country's true charm often lies just beyond the urban centres. Whether you're based in Edinburgh, Glasgow, Inverness, or Aberdeen, numerous day trips and excursions await, providing the perfect opportunity to immerse yourself in Scotland's breathtaking landscapes, rich history, and quaint villages. Below are some of the best day trips from major cities, each promising a memorable adventure.

1. Day Trips from Edinburgh

1.1. St. Andrews and the East Neuk of Fife

Just an hour's drive from Edinburgh, the historic town of St. Andrews is a must-visit for golf enthusiasts and history buffs alike. Explore the ruins of St. Andrews Cathedral, walk along the famous Old Course, and visit the University of St. Andrews, one of the oldest in the world. On your way back, take the coastal route through the East Neuk of Fife, where you can stop at charming fishing villages like Anstruther and Crail.

1.2. Rosslyn Chapel and the Pentland Hills

A short drive from Edinburgh, Rosslyn Chapel is a treasure trove of intricate carvings and mysterious history, made famous by The Da Vinci Code. After exploring the chapel, head to the nearby Pentland Hills Regional Park for a hike. The park offers trails for all levels, with stunning views of Edinburgh and the surrounding countryside.

1.3. The Borders Abbeys and Melrose

Venture south to the Scottish Borders, where you can visit the ruins of the region's famous abbeys—Melrose, Dryburgh, Kelso, and Jedburgh. Melrose Abbey, in particular, is said to be the burial place of Robert the Bruce's heart. After exploring the abbeys, spend some time in the charming town of Melrose, with its quaint shops and cafes.

2. Day Trips from Glasgow

2.1. Loch Lomond and The Trossachs National Park

Just a short drive from Glasgow, Loch Lomond and The Trossachs National Park is a natural wonderland. Spend the day hiking, biking, or boating in the park, or simply relax by the loch and enjoy the stunning scenery. For a more leisurely experience, take a cruise on Loch Lomond or visit the quaint village of Luss.

2.2. The Isle of Arran

Known as "Scotland in Miniature," the Isle of Arran offers a bit of everything, from rugged mountains to sandy beaches. Take the ferry from Ardrossan and spend the day exploring Brodick Castle, hiking Goatfell, or visiting the Arran Distillery. The island's compact size makes it ideal for a day trip.

2.3. Stirling and the Kelpies

An easy day trip from Glasgow, Stirling is home to the historic Stirling Castle and the nearby Wallace Monument. After exploring these iconic sites, continue to the Kelpies in Falkirk, towering horse-head sculptures that are a tribute to Scotland's industrial heritage. You can also visit the Falkirk Wheel, a unique rotating boat lift.

3. Day Trips from Inverness

3.1. Loch Ness and Urquhart Castle

No visit to Inverness is complete without a trip to Loch Ness. Spend the day exploring the loch, starting with a visit to the dramatic ruins of Urquhart Castle, perched on the loch's edge. Take a boat tour on the loch, keeping an eye out for the legendary Nessie, or hike along the Great Glen Way for stunning views of the water.

3.2. The Black Isle

A short drive from Inverness, the Black Isle is a peninsula known for its rolling farmland, charming villages, and wildlife. Visit the town of Cromarty, with its well-preserved Georgian architecture, and take a dolphin-spotting tour from Chanonry Point, one of the best places in Scotland to see these playful creatures.

3.3. Glen Affric

Glen Affric is often described as one of the most beautiful glens in Scotland, and it's easy to see why. Spend the day hiking through ancient Caledonian pine forests, alongside crystal-clear lochs, and beneath towering mountains. The area is a haven for wildlife, so keep an eye out for red deer, golden eagles, and pine martens.

4. Day Trips from Aberdeen

4.1. Royal Deeside and Balmoral Castle

Royal Deeside, west of Aberdeen, is famous for its connection to the British royal family. Visit Balmoral Castle, the Queen's Scottish residence, and explore the surrounding area, including the picturesque village of Braemar and the stunning Linn of Dee. The region also offers excellent hiking opportunities, particularly in the Cairngorms National Park.

4.2. Dunnottar Castle and Stonehaven

Perched on a dramatic clifftop overlooking the North Sea, Dunnottar Castle is one of Scotland's most iconic ruins. Spend the morning exploring the castle and then head to the nearby town of Stonehaven for a seafood lunch by the harbour. If you're feeling adventurous, take a walk along the coastal path for breathtaking views.

4.3. The Whisky Trail

Aberdeen is a great base for exploring the world-famous Whisky Trail in Speyside. Visit some of Scotland's most renowned distilleries, such as Glenfiddich, Macallan, and Glenlivet, where you can learn about the whisky-making process and enjoy a tasting. The scenic drive through the rolling hills of Speyside is a highlight in itself.

CHAPTER 10

FINAL TIPS AND RECOMMENDATIONS

Responsible Travel

Scotland is a country of immense natural beauty and cultural heritage, and it's essential to travel in a way that preserves its treasures for future generations. Here are some key tips on how to travel responsibly in Scotland:

Eco-Friendly Accommodations: Choose accommodations that prioritize sustainability, such as those with eco-certifications or practices like energy efficiency, waste reduction, and support for local communities.

Respecting Wildlife: Whether you're spotting dolphins on the coast or hiking in the Highlands, it's crucial to observe wildlife from a distance and follow guidelines to ensure their habitats are not disturbed.

Supporting Local Businesses: Eating at local restaurants, buying from local artisans, and participating in community-led tours not only enriches your experience but also supports the local economy and cultural preservation.

By making mindful choices, you can minimize your environmental impact while contributing positively to Scotland's local communities and natural environments.

What to Do in Case of...

Even the most meticulously planned trips can encounter unexpected challenges. Here's what to do in case you face common travel issues while in Scotland:

Lost Luggage: If your luggage doesn't arrive with you, report it immediately to the airline's desk at the airport. Keep a copy of your luggage claim ticket and ask for a reference number to track the status. Many airlines will cover essentials until your luggage is returned.

Medical Emergencies: For urgent medical issues, dial 999 for emergency services. If it's a non-urgent situation, you can visit a local GP (General Practitioner) or a pharmacy for advice. It's advisable to have travel insurance that covers medical expenses.

Car Breakdowns: If you're driving in Scotland and your car breaks down, contact your rental company or roadside assistance provider. Many rental companies offer 24/7 support. It's also a good idea to familiarize yourself with local road safety laws and carry an emergency kit in your car.

Weather-Related Disruptions: Scotland's weather can be unpredictable, particularly in rural or coastal areas. If severe weather affects your travel plans, stay updated with local news, heed any warnings, and consider having a flexible itinerary that allows for changes.

These practical tips will help you navigate and resolve any issues efficiently, ensuring that your trip continues smoothly despite any hiccups.

Conclusion

As you prepare to embark on your journey to Scotland, remember that the magic of travel lies not just in the places you visit but in the moments you create. Whether you're walking through the misty moors of the Highlands, exploring the ancient alleys of Edinburgh, or savouring a dram of whisky by a roaring fire, Scotland offers an experience that is both deeply personal and universally captivating.

This guide has equipped you with the knowledge, tips, and inspiration to make the most of your time in this remarkable country. But beyond the maps, itineraries, and practical advice, it's the unexpected encounters, the serendipitous discoveries, and the stories you'll bring back that will truly define your trip.

Scotland is a land of legends and landscapes, of history and hospitality. As you journey through its towns and countryside, may you find not just the beauty that fills postcards, but the warmth and spirit that makes Scotland unforgettable.

So pack your bags, set your compass, and let Scotland's charm unfold before you. Safe travels, and enjoy every moment of your adventure in the land of lochs, legends, and lasting memories.

Made in the USA
Las Vegas, NV
04 February 2025